"How does one release a logjam? We ask because there does seem to be a deadlock in certain conversations over liturgy these days. Geldhof proposes that we must look for that bottom log that is jamming things up, and for him that is not the impasse between left and right, it is rather a more radical issue: the relationship of sacred liturgy to the secular world. Utilizing an array of philosophers and interpreters of culture, he challenges the definition of secularism with which we work; utilizing an array of historians and liturgists, he challenges our epistemological approach to liturgy in favor of a soteriological one. The result is not a modernized liturgy, but a liturgy that functions in our modern lives."

—David W. Fagerberg
University of Notre Dame

"Setting liturgical experience in critical dialogue with the current cultural moment—using the deepest insights of the liturgical movement to elucidate the former while using philosophy, anthropology, and the history of ideas to make clear the latter—Joris Geldhof has borne witness to a liturgical theology that joins together matters that are frequently divorced: church and world, cult and culture, heaven and earth, religion and politics, God's future and the present age. This learned, wise, and clearly-written book invites us again to a dense celebration of the liturgy as a complex of symbols that can save us all from the loneliness and isolation belonging to ideological secularism, while refusing to reject secularity itself. Both progressive and conservative, this lovely book affirms the world while welcoming God's urgently needed salvation."

—Gordon W. Lathrop
Professor of Liturgy Emeritus, United Lutheran Seminary of Pennsylvania
Past-President, Societas Liturgica and Past-President, North American Academy of Liturgy

D1519483

"Pulling together a decade of scholarly research and essays into a single book, Joris Geldhof brings to a wider audience a much-needed application of social-philosophical theory to move analysis of the weakening force of liturgy in late-modernity beyond the tired polemics of so-called traditionalist versus reformist church politics to a deeper understanding of the fundamental challenges yet unique potential for liturgical practice today."

    —Bruce T. Morrill, SJ
    Vanderbilt University

Liturgy and Secularism

Beyond the Divide

Joris Geldhof

LITURGICAL PRESS
ACADEMIC

Collegeville, Minnesota
www.litpress.org

Cover design by Tara Wiese.

1	2	3	4	5	6	7	8	9

Library of Congress Cataloging-in-Publication Data

Names: Geldhof, Joris, 1976– author.
Title: Liturgy and secularism : beyond the divide / Joris Geldhof.
Description: Collegeville, Minnesota : Liturgical Press, 2018. | "A
   Liturgical Press Academic book." | Includes bibliographical
   references.
Identifiers: LCCN 2018004074 (print) | LCCN 2018030513 (ebook) |
   ISBN 9780814684863 (ebook) | ISBN 9780814684610
Subjects: LCSH: Liturgics. | Public worship. | Secularism.
Classification: LCC BV178 (ebook) | LCC BV178 .G45 2018 (print) |
   DDC 264—dc23
LC record available at https://lccn.loc.gov/2018004074

To the memory of Wouter

Contents

Acknowledgments

I owe a great deal of gratitude to many people who, together, but each in their own way, have made it possible for this book to come into being. First, I would like to thank those students and colleagues—but also friends and family—who asked me intriguing questions about how liturgy (still) relates to the culture in which we live. Questions on this and related topics are difficult ones to address, but through these conversations, which often provoke uneasiness, I have, above all, been blessed to learn a lot.

In particular, I thank my colleagues at the Faculty of Theology and Religious Studies of KU Leuven with whom I am involved in the GOA research project, "The Crisis of Religion and the Problem of Roman Catholic Self-Definition," Terrence, Mathijs, Wim, and Lieven. This book is situated at the very heart of our investigations and initiatives. Particular thanks are also due to my dear colleague Thomas, of the Liturgical Institute at KU Leuven, which we chair together, and to my past and current Ph.D. students, the conversations with whom I cherish more than they probably imagine: Bilju, Colman, Duco, Frédérique, Geert, Jaya, Jobin, Johan, Joshy G., Joshy P., Liju, Maryann, Maura, Nepo, Olivier, Philippe, Richard, Roshan, Sam, Sebeesh, Serge, Sojan, Tom, Trevor, and Victoria.

Second, I must thank those who have organized the conferences, workshops, and colloquia where I have had the opportunity to present my ideas and to engage in stimulating discussions and debates. Thanks are also owed to those who urged and invited me to publish articles and essays and to those who practically enabled these activities. I wish to express my sincere gratitude to those editors who have generously allowed that previously published work may appear here in this book, albeit always in slightly modified forms. A particular word of thanks is due to Julia, who translated the basic text of chapter 2 from German to English, and to Trevor, who was so kind to proofread the entire volume.

Third, it is only but appropriate that I express a special word of thanks to Karen, Sien, and Noor, my wife and daughters. Without the daily conversations about life, school, jobs, friends, and the world at large—the important things as well as those which sometimes seem less so—there would not have been a single reason, let alone the motivation, to compose this book.

Joris Geldhof
August 2017

Provenance of the Chapters

The first sections of chapter 1 are based largely on an article, "Liturgy, Modernity, and Ideology: Reflections on Similarities and Differences between Trent and Vatican II," in *Asian Horizons* 7 (2015): 178–87. Sections of the second part of this chapter are taken from the seventh chapter in a collective volume in which the papers presented at the third Sacra Liturgica conference, which took place in London in July 2016, were published: Uwe M. Lang, ed., *Authentic Liturgical Renewal in Contemporary Perspective* (London: Bloomsbury T. & T. Clark, 2017): 83–95.

The greater part of chapter 2 is a translation and slight adaptation of a contribution in German published in *Erbe und Erneuerung: Die Liturgiekonstitution des Zweiten Vatikanischen Konzils und ihre Folgen*, edited by Hans-Jürgen Feulner, Andreas Bieringer, and Benjamin Leven, Österreichische Studien zur Liturgiewissenschaft und Sakramententheologie 7 (Wien: Lit, 2015): 121–35. The title of the original contribution was "Wieviel Säkularisierung verträgt die Liturgie? Kulturphilosophische und liturgietheologische Erwägungen."

Chapter 3 was originally an article in French, "Sacré, salut et liturgie. À la rencontre de la théologie et de l'anthropologie," which appeared in the journal of the Institut Catholique de Paris, *Transversalités* 112 (2009): 19–37. Here and there, while translating, I made a couple of minor changes and additions to the text.

Chapter 4 is almost identical to an article, "Liturgy: From Desacralization to Sanctification," which was published in the *Yearbook of Ritual and Liturgical Studies* 31 (2015): 117–31.

Chapter 5 is entirely based on new material and has not been published elsewhere. The inspiration for it came from a course I taught in the Spring of 2017.

The groundwork for chapter 6 was laid in two contributions, the first of which was originally a lecture I gave in the context of the Eucharistic Congress in Dublin in 2012: "The End of the Mass for the Masses? Reflections on the Source and Summit of the Christian Life of Faith in Secular Cultures," in *50ᵗʰ International Eucharistic Congress—Proceedings of the International Symposium of Theology: The Ecclesiology of Communion Fifty Years after the Opening of Vatican II* (Dublin: Veritas, 2013): 624–41. The second contribution was originally a lecture too, which I delivered at a symposium about Eucharist and communion in Trichur, Kerala (India), in the summer of 2014. The title of my talk was "Becoming the Body of Christ: Preliminary Attempts at a Eucharistic Synthesis (Rereading Dom Lambert Beauduin's *La piété de l'église*)," and it was published in *Encounter: A Journal of Interdisciplinary Reflections of Faith and Life* 6 (2015): 25–41. Large portions of both these texts were taken over without any change.

Introduction

This book sets itself an ambitious goal. It attempts to do three different things at the same time. First, it aims to undermine certain assumptions about the relation and the interaction between the life of worship of the church on the one hand, and the secular cultures in which this happens on the other hand. For much too long, liturgists and theologians have looked at the relationship between liturgy and secularization in a narrow and too schematic mode—which often resulted in unnecessary antagonisms, oppositions, and even downright hostility. It is all too often supposed that in embracing secular culture, one must to some extent let go of liturgy, or conversely, that in choosing for liturgy one must close the door on secular culture. One of the major objectives of the present book is to show that these patterns of thinking can and should be left behind if one is genuinely concerned about the future of Christian faith—regardless of whether one opts (rather) for liturgy or for secular culture.

Second, the reflections I offer in this book are intended to contribute to a deeper insight into the nature of the liturgy. What the liturgy actually is and does is notoriously difficult to grasp. There is by no means any lack of definitions and descriptions of liturgy, but most do little more than emphasize a single—or perhaps a few—dimensions of it. As such, there is nothing wrong with that—in a way, such inquiries have to be undertaken, at least for pedagogical reasons—but the conceptual strategies behind the formulations of these definitions are always limited. Worse is when the liturgy is reduced to another phenomenon, as if it can ever be considered simply one element of a set. In such approaches, liturgy is considered a conglomeration of rituals, a rhythmed practice of worship, the church's self-expression par excellence, etc. Or else the liturgy is compared to and set in a relation with similar phenomena, such as popular devotion, *diakonia*, catechesis, tradition, a tool for evangelization, theatrical performance, inculturation, etc. The problem with these reductions and comparisons is not that they are unhelpful but that each contains an in-built tendency toward one-sidedness. In this book I aim to overcome some of these intrinsic risks which generally do little justice to the liturgy itself.

Third, I want to continue interdisciplinary and ecumenical conversations about the liturgy, which can meaningfully be regarded as the most precious treasure Christians carry on their journey through the *saecula*, the centuries. It is not my intention to offer a comprehensive theory or to voice a straightforward opinion. Rather, I intend to stimulate the ongoing dialogue between "faith" and "culture" from the very specific, but at the same time, general and encompassing, perspective of the worship practices of Christians. It is clear to me that this dialogue, both qua content and qua form, goes beyond the scope of individual skills as well as beyond the reach of clear-cut methods and scientific disciplines. Therefore, it is not a disadvantage but an asset of this book that it cuts through different fields and that it strives to embrace different competences. Basically, of course, it is a piece of writing which belongs to the area of liturgical theology, but to the extent that this is true, the book itself integrates insights from the history of ideas, fundamental and systematic theology, symbol theories, philosophies of culture, anthropology, ritual studies, and more. The book does not claim any specialized scholarship in any of these fields. Rather, what it seeks to convey is only possible through a combination of ideas from all these disciplines.

For the structure of this book, inspiration has been drawn from a diptych. Diptychs—usually small, double-miniature paintings that can be opened and closed and easily taken along on a journey—were made to nurture personal piety and prayer. They normally depicted two different but related mysteries of faith, and they were keenly cherished by their possessors. Most important, however, is that one cannot have one panel without the other. One panel on its own makes little sense; deepening one's insights only comes about through continuous and perspicuous meditation on both. One must regard one panel and then the other, meditating on each, always again shifting one's gaze and attention. Only if one perseveres with these practices does one come to a profound insight into the work—one based not on hasty deductions but on quiet contemplation.

The two panels of the diptych of the present book are inspired by the double need to locate liturgy and the world in and through each other. Underlying is the assumption that one cannot overcome the regrettable divide between liturgy and secularism unless a series of deeper reflections about the manifold relations of liturgy and world is carried out. In other words, just as it is the case with the practice of prayer with the help of a diptych, one has to look long and carefully at liturgy and long and carefully at the world and thereby shift the attention from the one to the other many times. This method of repeated attention and discipline leads to a point where one realizes that one cannot have the one without the other—or in this case, that one panel cannot present a "world" without the liturgy being part of it, and that the other cannot present "liturgy" without the world being intrinsically involved it.

Correspondingly, the first part of this book is entitled "positioning the liturgy in the world" and the second one "positioning the world in the liturgy." One understands liturgy better if one does not consider it an isolated phenomenon that is detached from its ties with culture and society and the human beings inhabiting them. And, at least as a Christian, though not exclusively, one understands secularism better if one looks at that culture and society from within the "world" of the liturgy. Moreover, the two parts of this book each start with a motto, each of which is purposely taken from *Sacrosanctum Concilium*. The reasons for doing this will hopefully become clear throughout the book and will also be explicitly elucidated in the general conclusion.

The two parts of the book each comprise three chapters of approximately equal length. Each chapter contributes in its own way to the major points I make. The first chapter takes a look at the history of ideas and tries to disentangle notions that are too often confused: modernity, secularism, rationalism, and Enlightenment. That they are not the same and that the liturgy of the church does not need to be threatened by any of them is an insight of utmost importance. The second chapter more concretely discusses the relation between liturgy, society, modern culture, and politics. It is argued that liturgy is not only a victim of ideologies but that it can—and actually should—play a proactive and leading role in the de-ideologization of many modern(ist) and secular(ist) discourses. The third chapter takes its point of departure in anthropology and delves into the complex issue of the relation between the sacred and the profane. I develop the idea that the liturgy does not side with either of these but that it brings a new, and renewing, perspective in both.

This very idea is pursued in the fourth chapter, where the undeniable desacralizing tendency of Christian faith in general, and liturgy in particular, is further explored. The findings of these reflections result in affirming the universal sanctifying dynamics and the eschatological nature of Christian liturgies. The fifth chapter seeks more detailed theological support for this claim, in that it aims at retrieving some wisdom from key figures representing the twentieth century liturgical movement in Europe. Scholars from this movement had a fine sense for a widespread liturgical "crisis" and tried to turn the tide in a difficult ecclesial and intellectual climate. Upon close inspection, it seems that many of their insights and proposals are surprisingly pertinent for today, and it is therefore worth remembering what they were up to. The sixth and final chapter, then, is a reflection on the liturgy's critical potential. The guiding question of this chapter is how good liturgy can continue to inspire and shape the church and the world in a time where the Eucharist is no longer the Mass for the masses.

At the end of these introductory observations it is only appropriate that I inform the reader about my own context. I am a forty-one year old white Roman Catholic layperson who grew up in a middle-class family in an ordinary town in the Flemish-speaking part of Belgium. I was baptized as an infant, did first communion at the age of six (the first year of primary school) and was confirmed at the age of eleven (the last year of primary school). The schools I went to and the churches my parents took me to for these events, as well as for weekly Mass, were located within a radius of less than one kilometer. The shape of the Eucharist with which I have been familiar since my childhood is the parish Sunday Mass with one priest presiding, celebrated (more or less) according to the Roman Rite.

Today I live in the city of Ghent, which has served as the seat of a diocese since the sixteenth century and where the impressive St. Bavo's Cathedral houses *The Adoration of the Lamb* (probably more frequently called the Ghent Altarpiece), painted by the Van Eyck brothers. It is a particular pleasure and privilege to view this magnificent piece of art that has stood the test of the centuries and is currently being restored. Every now and then I go to St. Bavo's to contemplate the piece or to introduce guests and visitors to its intriguing iconographic program, colors, figures, and composition.

One of the things that these visits to the cathedral and its famous polyptych have taught me is that, when reflecting on the nature, the meaning, and the relevance of liturgy and

Eucharist, one's context is important but certainly not determinant. Therefore, I dare to hope that my reflections on Christian worship and secularization and about how to overcome the divide between liturgy and secularism are pertinent for people from other regions and cultures, from other churches, from other ages, and from other rites. Notwithstanding the understandable temptations, both intellectual and cultural, of particularisms and relativisms, I still hold on to a firm universalism when it comes to defending the significance of Christian liturgy and sacraments. Some of the reasons for this universalism and its underlying metaphysics will become apparent in the following chapters.

PART I

Positioning the Liturgy in the World

In the earthly liturgy we take part in a foretaste of that heavenly liturgy which is celebrated in the holy city of Jerusalem toward which we journey as pilgrims, where Christ is sitting at the right hand of God, minister of the sanctuary and of the true tabernacle . . . With all the hosts of heaven we sing a hymn of glory to the Lord; venerating the memory of the saints, we hope to share their company; we eagerly await the Saviour, Our Lord Jesus Christ, until he our life shall appear and we too will appear with him in glory.

—*Sacrosanctum Concilium* 8

CHAPTER 1

Liturgy, Modernity and Secularization

One often hears that the Roman Catholic Church only opened its windows to the modern world at Vatican II. This is a curious statement, however, for it supposes an understanding of modernity which may be radically questioned—and for good reason. In actuality, it means that the church had missed the boat of contemporary (Western) society for a very long time. At the same time, it implied the hope that the church would soon adopt a (more) democratic culture, that church-leaders would attach (more) importance to the idea that every baptized person is an equal member of the church understood as the peregrinating people of God, and that corresponding proposals would be implemented to modify procedures of decision-making in the church at large. When it comes to the liturgical life of the church, this position usually favors the active participation of all the faithful in worship services of all kinds, celebrations of the Eucharist, the sacraments and the Liturgy of the Hours in vernacular languages, and an overall easy access to the church's ritual and ceremonial repertoire.

In the first part of this chapter, I do not want to challenge the pertinence or the value of these ideas in the contemporary context, but I do want to challenge the understanding of modernity that often underlies them. In particular, I intend to criticize the assumption that changes in the church's worship must be made (only) because of prevailing ideas or shifting sensitivities in society and culture, for example, under the influence of a set of convictions broadly shared by the majority of the people. To build up my argument in an appropriate manner, I first briefly compare the liturgical reforms issuing from the Council of Trent and Vatican II, which is a meaningful exercise if one realizes that the time between these epoch-making church gatherings largely coincides with the era in which modernity and secularization grew. On the basis of this comparison I will make a suggestion for what I think is a more fruitful understanding of the interplay between liturgy and secularisation.

In the second part of the chapter, I shift the attention to the present situation while further developing the thesis that liturgy and secularisation do not mutually exclude each other. I argue that it is both unfruitful and unnecessary to defend or assume the position that, if you are secular, you cannot be reasonably religious, and the reverse, that if you are religious, you ought to be against secularization. The fact is that both of these positions, and the many variations of them on the spectrum between "extremely religious" and "extremely secular" misunderstand the nature of Christian sacramentality.[1] For Christian sacramentality, inasmuch as it is liturgical,[2] does not allow itself to be caught in any binary opposition.

1. A Look at History: Trent and Vatican II

Post-Tridentine Liturgical Reforms

As a matter of fact, Trent entertained a paradoxical relation with the liturgy. It was above all preoccupied with a theoretical-

---

1. For a recent selection of thought-provoking reflections about this, see Lizette Larson-Miller, *Sacramentality Renewed: Contemporary Conversations in Sacramental Theology* (Collegeville, MN: Liturgical Press, 2016).

2. In this sense I fully align myself with David Fagerberg, for whom "sacraments are liturgical" and "liturgy is sacramental." See "Liturgy, Signs, and Sacraments," in *The Oxford Handbook of Sacramental Theology*, ed. Hans Boersma and Mathew Levering (Oxford: Oxford University Press, 2015), 455–65.

theological understanding of the sacraments and defended classical doctrines over and against what it thought were aberrations in the thinking and writings of representatives of the Reformation. Trent did not deal with the liturgy in an equally profound way as it did in the realm of the theology of the sacraments. In an article published long before he became the secretary of the *Consilium ad exsequendam Constitutionem de Sacra Liturgia*, Annibale Bugnini observed that the term "liturgy" itself is almost completely absent from the council's canons and decrees.[3] This observation goes beyond the level of the anecdotic and the semantic. Paraphrasing the famous words of prominent liturgical theologian and American Benedictine Aidan Kavanagh, for Trent, orthodoxy seemed to denote first and foremost "doctrinal accuracy" and only secondarily "right worship."[4] In a very apologetic way, Trent stipulated what to think and, even more pointedly, how not to think about the sacraments. Its understanding of liturgy was, all in all, a very superficial one—related in its entirety to the church's solemn ceremonies as performed by the priestly class.

A good example of a general assessment of Trent's position towards liturgy is provided by the famous Austrian liturgical scholar and spokesperson of the liturgical movement Josef Andreas Jungmann. Jungmann appeals to the general reputation of the council as a "reform" council and says that the council actually had a quite restricted notion of "reform," which it above all interpreted as the condemnation and correction of abuses.[5] In addition, the council wanted to restore

3. Annibale Bugnini, "La 'liturgia' dei sacramenti al concilio di Trento," in *Ephemerides Liturgicae* 59 (1945): 39–51.

4. Aidan Kavanagh, *Introduction to Liturgical Theology* (Collegeville, MN: Liturgical Press, 1992), 3.

5. This standard interpretation of the Council of Trent is to a large extent the merit of Hubert Jedin's monumental five-volume study entitled *History of the Council of Trent* (original German version: *Geschichte des Konzils von Trient*, Freiburg: Herder, 1949–1975).

the liturgy to a more ancient, unspoiled model.[6] However, it
lacked the knowledge and the means to effectuate such an
ideal because of the simple fact that historico-liturgical scholarship had not yet come up with a full understanding of the
development of the Roman Rite in the sixteenth century.[7] This
implies that the council understood the liturgy's original form
ideologically: liturgy represented a normative vision which
had to be rigorously implemented, and along with that implementation came rigorous inspection and surveillance.

Because of the emphatic lack of interest in the liturgy qua
liturgy, historical scholars have suggested that the most important Tridentine accomplishments pertaining to the liturgy
are neither to be situated in what the council fathers said in
the documents they produced nor during the council itself,
but only afterwards through the popes and the commissions
they assigned. In this respect, Nathan Mitchell rightly observes: "Strictly speaking, neither Trent nor Vatican II 're-
formed' Roman Catholic worship. Instead, each called for the
creation of papally appointed commissions to carry out the

6. Joseph A. Jungmann, "Das Konzil von Trient und die Erneuerung
der Liturgie," in *Das Weltkonzil von Trient. Sein Werden und Wirken*, ed.
Georg Schreiber (Freiburg: Herder, 1951), 325–36, 325: "Gerade auf litur-
gischem Gebiet war die Aufgabe des Konzils die Reform, und zwar
Reform in dem engeren Sinn der Beseitigung von Mißbräuchen und der
Rückkehr zu einer älteren, von Mißbildungen noch freien 'Form.' "
    7. This point is made, among others, by Martin Klöckener and Angelus
Häußling in their respective commentaries on the bull *Quo primum* pro-
mulgating the 1570 missal and on the phenomenon of liturgical reform
as a challenge for liturgical studies. See also Martin Klöckener, "Die Bulle
'Quo primum' Papst Pius' V vom 14. Juli 1570 zur Promulgation des
nachtridentinischen *Missale Romanum*," in *Archiv für Liturgiewissenschaft*
48 (2006): 41–51; Angelus Häußling, "Liturgiereform. Materialien zu
einem neuen Thema der Liturgiewissenschaft," in *Archiv für Liturgiewissenschaft* 31 (1989): 1–32.

task."[8] It seems that the post-Tridentine liturgical reforms are the consequence of drastic changes in the self-organization of the church rather than the fruit of a profound reflection on what the liturgy and its church-building potentials are.

In addition, these historical scholars consistently mention the establishment of the Sacred Congregation of Rites by Pope Sixtus V in 1588 and the publication of the major liturgical books: the *Breviarium Romanum* in 1568, the *Missale Romanum* in 1570, the *Pontificale Romanum* in 1595–96, and the *Rituale Romanum* in 1614.[9] One could legitimately defend the idea that the whole process that drove these initiatives was decidedly modern and no less ideologically motivated. The church set up a bureaucratic organ which aimed at a doctrinal uniformity and a liturgical standardization of gigantic proportions, employed efficient means to control both of them, and seemed unwilling to give any room for spontaneity. In the time span roughly between the end of the sixteenth and the end of the nineteenth centuries, the liturgy and the life of worship and devotion of Roman Catholic faithful had become officialized in a way unparalleled in the entire history of Christianity. Whether this was a truly "liturgical" reform, as one often assumes, is a serious question to which there is no easy answer. But there are serious reasons for doubt about it.[10]

8. Nathan Mitchell says this in the preface to James F. White, *Roman Catholic Worship: Trent to Today*, 2nd ed. (Collegeville, MN: Liturgical Press, 2003), x.

9. For some background to this development in the promulgation of liturgical books, see my forthcoming contribution, "Trent and the Production of Liturgical Books in its Aftermath," in *The Council of Trent: Reform and Controversy in Europe and Beyond (1545–1700), vol. 1: Between Trent, Rome and Wittenberg*, ed. Wim François and Violet Soen (Göttingen: Vandenhoeck & Ruprecht, 2017).

10. In this respect, see my article, "Did the Council of Trent Produce a Liturgical Reform? The Case of the Roman Missal," in *Questions Liturgiques/Studies in Liturgy* 93 (2012): 171–95.

Post-Vatican II Liturgical Reforms

There are a number of similarities between the liturgical reforms after Trent and the ones carried out by the *Consilium ad exsequendam Constitutionem de Sacra Liturgia*, which came into being during the Second Vatican Council.[11] This led to the creation of a special commission aimed at more efficiently implementing the council's decisions, including organizing the administrative, legal, and practical necessities associated with these tasks. Though a certain degree of experimentation was allowed for, these experiments were always neatly controlled by church officials, who administrated them as scientists do in their laboratories. The fact that there was some room for experimentation did not imply that any individual or group of people could simply establish its own version of liturgical celebrations or that liturgical innovations would henceforth depend on the creativity and authenticity of those groups and their leaders. To the contrary, there were clear criteria and procedures and there was an admirably well-organized system of reporting and approving.[12] Most interestingly, there was a widely shared anxiety for and even a refusal of inner diversity. The goal was to carry out the liturgical reforms as quickly and as efficiently as possible, everywhere. That sounds very much like the operational logic of an ideology.

The question is whether these similarities between the post-Vatican II and post-Tridentine liturgical reforms must not be counterbalanced by their differences. I think that this is the case, and I also think it is timely and important to stress these

11. Piero Marini, *A Challenging Reform: Realizing the Vision of the Liturgical Renewal 1963–1975* (Collegeville, MN: Liturgical Press, 2007).

12. The standard work that chronicles the works of the *Consilium* is still Annibale Bugnini, *The Reform of the Liturgy, 1948–1975*, trans. Matthew J. O'Connell (Collegeville, MN: Liturgical Press, 1990).

differences.[13] Let me elaborate upon this idea with three arguments that mutually reinforce one another.

First, the substance and the nature of the liturgy were explicitly addressed by the Second Vatican Council. This was the first council in the entire history of the church that devoted explicit attention to the liturgy qua liturgy. The liturgy was given due theological, spiritual, and pastoral weight beyond merely theoretical and juridical concerns. When one carefully reads *Sacrosanctum Concilium*, it is striking that so much theological and spiritual attention is given to the liturgy and how Scripture is employed to underpin and underscore these claims. The general guidelines and practical proposals flow forth from a fundamental reflection on the position, the value, and—above all—the immense importance of the liturgy in the life of the

13. Within the confines of this book I do not want to engage myself in discussions around the "reform of the reform" movement and the far-reaching criticisms launched against the post-Vatican II liturgical reforms by some rightist opposition groups. For a work representative of this current, see László Dobszay, *The Bugnini-Liturgy and the Reform of the Reform* (Front Royal: Catholic Church Music Associates, 2003), as well as the second large publication by the same author about the same subject matter, *The Restoration and Organic Development of the Roman Rite* (London: T. & T. Clark, 2010). In some of the rhetoric, Dobszay seems to have difficulties with the "creative will of commissions" (*The Bugnini-Liturgy*, 9) that changed the liturgy, because what they did was not in line with the organic development of the liturgy. It remains quite unclear what Dobszay exactly means by this but he somehow understands it as the age-old traditional expression of the way in which God's people ritually responds to God's salvific initiative. Dobszay apparently aims at "modern" and "secular" evolutions when he is criticizing the post-Vatican II liturgical renewal, but he never gives a sufficient explanation of how he interprets these concepts. Therefore, it is legitimate not to deal with his ideas in the framework of the present book. A well-informed and balanced study about these (and other) critiques is John F. Baldovin, *Reforming the Liturgy: A Response to the Critics* (Collegeville, MN: Liturgical Press, 2008).

church.[14] One looks in vain for such a robust treatment of the liturgy and its biblical roots in Trent's canons and decrees.

Second, this theological approach to liturgy made it possible for the church to redefine itself in its relation to God, his revelation and his covenant, and to redefine the community that tries to live up to his commandment of universal love. Trent had not interpreted these realities in such a way, at least partially because of the polemical context it saw itself confronted with. Whereas Vatican II adopted a genuinely ecumenical and much more irenic approach, Trent reacted to a context which it interpreted to be inimical.[15] Moreover, a convincing case has been made that the liturgical and ecumenical dimensions of Vatican II were intrinsically connected, that is, not two distinct issues with which the council fathers dealt.[16]

Third, the program of concrete liturgical reforms was intrinsically motivated. Vatican II preferred the concept of renewal (*renovatio*) and meant by it a comprehensive conversion of the church as Body of Christ and God's people, much more than the adaptation of rubrics in view of preserving an amalgamate of ritual and textual traditions. The liturgical reform was

14. This reading of the preeminent importance of the council's theology of the liturgy is in line with Massimo Faggioli's groundbreaking study: *True Reform: Liturgy and Ecclesiology in* Sacrosanctum Concilium (Collegeville, MN: Liturgical Press, 2012). There is little doubt that this book is one of the most important studies when it comes to interpreting and valuing the liturgical reforms brought about by the council.

15. Some conservative groups tend to look down on Vatican II's deliberately "pastoral" approach and contrast the pastoral nature of a council with a "dogmatic" one. That such an opposition of these categories is absurd and that the underlying assumption, namely, that being "pastoral" would be less important, less valuable, or less legitimate, is bare nonsense, is eloquently demonstrated by Ephrem Carr, "*Sacrosanctum concilium* and its Consequences: The Reform of the Liturgy," *Questions Liturgiques/Studies in Liturgy* 92 (2011): 183–94.

16. Again, this interpretation resonates with Faggioli, *True Reform*.

understood as an engine, not as an accident. If at all Trent produced a liturgical reform, it was rather the result of an ecclesial reorganization both *ad intra* and *ad extra* than the fruit of a reflection about its deepest calling in and for the world.

Similarities and Differences between Trent and Vatican II

The most ardent defenders of the post-Vatican II liturgical reforms have not always clearly distinguished between the theoretical and practical ideals of the liturgical movement on the one hand and the profound theological understanding of the liturgy of Vatican II on the other. This explains why there has been a great deal of aggression, frustration, and seemingly unbridgeable misunderstandings in the aftermath. Therefore, I think it is timely and important to patiently discern what is ideology and what is theology. To read Trent as a modern council and to realize that Vatican II equally has modern traits can be helpful in that kind of exercise. However, the real challenge more than half a century after the promulgation of *Sacrosanctum Concilium* may not be to win the battle over the right interpretation of the document but to interiorize the thoroughly theological sense of liturgy it promoted. It is my conviction that such a reading may be instrumental to overcome one-sided interpretations of the constitution and to move beyond the question of whether the council embraced modernity or not, and whether that embracement was a good thing or not. Let us now see what this perspective could entail for an exploration of the present context.

2. An Exploration of the Present Situation

Situating the Secular

To explain what secularism means is to look at the intellectual heritage of Western culture. According to widespread anthropological theories, every civilization knows about a difference between the sacred and the profane.[17] It seems impossible that sacredness could determine every moment of one's life, just as it seems equally unthinkable that one could operate entirely and exclusively from birth to death in the atmosphere of the profane. In other words, there must be rupture and difference if life is to be livable. However, according to renowned scholars, in Western societies, the very conditions of this difference changed drastically with the rise of modernity. The traditional equilibrium between the metaphysical triad of the world, the soul, and God was shaken when autonomous subjectivity took the lead both in the acquisition process of knowledge and in judging good and evil.[18]

This slow but thoroughgoing revolution in epistemology and ethics, and from there in many other areas of life, evidently occasioned fundamental reinterpretations of faith and religion. The Flemish-American philosopher of culture and religion Louis Dupré observes: "The anthropocentric position has installed itself solidly in the modern mind. The turn to the subject, once taken, cannot be unmade. Yet it need not result in the reductionist conclusions that secularism has drawn from it."[19] It seems, therefore, that variations of a middle position are necessary to cope with the present crisis of Christianity, and a fortiori Catholicism, in secular environments. Before we go any further, however, it is preferable to continue to specify what secularism means.

---

17. Mircea Eliade, *The Sacred and the Profane: The Nature of Religion* (New York: Harper and Row, 1961).

18. See the trilogy of Louis Dupré, *Passage to Modernity: An Essay in the Hermeneutics of Nature and Culture* (New Haven: Yale University Press, 1993); *The Enlightenment and the Intellectual Foundations of Modern Culture* (New Haven: Yale University Press, 2004); and *The Quest of the Absolute: Birth and Decline of European Romanticism* (Notre Dame: University of Notre Dame Press, 2013).

19. Louis Dupré, *Symbols of the Sacred* (Grand Rapids, MI: Eerdmans, 2000), 126.

The famous Canadian philosopher Charles Taylor reminds one of the etymology of the term. It is "a category that developed within Latin Christendom. First, it was one term of a dyad. The secular had to do with the 'century'—that is, with profane time—and it was contrasted with what related to the eternal, or to sacred time."[20] Later on, roughly from the seventeenth century onwards, Taylor holds, the meaning of the concept of *saeculum* was significantly extended. The contrast was no longer with another temporal dimension, in which "spiritual" institutions had their niche; rather, the secular was, in its new sense, opposed to any claim made in the name of something transcendent of this world and its interests.[21] This enlargement of the meaning of the word and the fact that it was no longer seen as one component of a dyad, had radical consequences: "secular and religious are opposed as true and false or necessary and superfluous. The goal of policy becomes, in many cases, to abolish one while conserving the other."[22]

In a way similar to Dupré, Taylor sees the problem with secularism and its stance towards religion not as an intrinsic evil. The real problem is that secularism often goes along with a certain kind of reductionism or exclusivism: it focuses only on certain aspects of human conscience, intelligence, society, science, culture, etc. and refuses to see simultaneously "other dimensions." Dupré explains:

> The modern age has transferred the primary source of meaning and value from nature, and thus ultimately, from the Creator of nature, to the human mind. Any reality other than that of the mind itself becomes thereby reduced to the status of an object. But once the constitution

20. Charles Taylor, "What Does Secularism Mean?," in *Dilemmas and Connections: Selected Essays* (Cambridge, MA: The Belknap Press of Harvard University Press, 2011), 304.

21. Taylor, "What Does Secularism Mean?," 304.

22. Taylor, "What Does Secularism Mean?," 307.

of "objectivity" has become the principal function of the
mind, the mind itself ends up possessing no content of
its own. . . . The self has become a mere function of its
own mental acts.[23]

Or, in other words, the self has become fundamentally *lonely*.
Nevertheless, it remains possible to develop visions on humanity and divinity and the ways they interact with each other
within a context determined by modern secular conditions.
The task, Taylor suggests, is "taking our modern civilization
for another of those great cultural forms that have come and
gone in human history, to see what it means to be a Christian
here, to find our authentic voice in the eventual Catholic
chorus."[24] My own additional suggestion would be that nothing but the liturgy, substantially understood, is primordial in
this exercise of discernment.

From a meta point of view, it is interesting to observe that
there has been a shift from the temporal to the spatial in the
meaning of secularism. The secular now refers above all to the
space or the room within which we live today. It has become
the fundamental quality of the environment of life; it determines the very coordinates of where we are. We cannot situate
ourselves unless we refer to the secular conditions of our *Lebenswelt*. Yet, it has become fashionable in some circles to use
the concept of the "post-secular." This usage supposes that the
secular is something which determines a certain period of time
and that this time has come to an end. It is indeed the conviction of several scholars that the concept of the secular no longer

23. Louis Dupré, *Religion and the Rise of Modern Culture* (Notre Dame:
University of Notre Dame Press, 2008), 114–15.
24. Charles Taylor, "A Catholic Modernity?," in *Dilemmas and Connections: Selected Essays* (Cambridge, MA: The Belknap Press of Harvard
University Press, 2011), 169.

adequately captures the nature of our time and that, in the meantime, a new era has emerged.

Whether or not one believes this is true, of course, largely depends on one's interpretation of the secular. Inasmuch as the secularization hypothesis—which predicted the disappearance of religion as the necessary impact of scientific, technological, economic, and democratic expansion—was enfeebled, there is definitely something to say in favor of a discourse about the post-secular.[25] But just as it is the case with the relationship between modernity and postmodernism, the post-secular does not bring along something substantially different vis-à-vis secularism. In particular, post-secular conditions do not miraculously occasion the rebirth of religion and faith or a revival of a natural sense of sacredness. In any case, the fate of such revivals is largely irrelevant to the question of liturgical renewal. Christian liturgy does not exist to nourish a sense of the sacred but to sanctify the world and to worship God.

A Topography of Liturgy

In line with these meditations on the nature and meaning of secularism, we now shift our attention to the liturgy. We saw that secularism must be understood as a confluence of factors that deeply impact the very space and time in which we live. As a matter of fact, such is also true of the liturgy. Therefore, instead of asking ourselves *what* the liturgy is, I propose we approach the matter from a radically different angle, asking instead *where* is the liturgy, and *when* is the liturgy? In changing our focus thus, we may leave behind the

25. For an interesting conceptual exploration of this concept, see Arie L. Molendijk, "In Pursuit of the Postsecular," in *International Journal of Philosophy and Theology* 76 (2016): 100–15. Also the other contributions to this special issue are devoted to the issue of the post-secular as a challenge for contemporary theology and worth reading.

logics of definition, classification, and categorization as we know them and begin to make time and space for a topography and chronography of liturgy.

To refuse to start from a definition of the liturgy is in a way to deviate, albeit slightly, though no less deliberately, from a method that was often applied in the bosom of the liturgical movement. Major representatives of that movement have come up with intriguing and encompassing definitions of the church's liturgical worship, but in doing so, they thereby inscribed themselves into a logic of division-making which I think the liturgy itself actually challenges. There were, of course, important pastoral and contextual reasons for distinguishing between private prayer and collective devotional practices on the one hand and the "official" liturgy of the church on the other hand.[26] However, instead of making subtle distinctions, many theoreticians of the liturgy ended up drawing harsh demarcations and thereby, sadly, further instantiated pre-existing separations. Today, I think that the problem is no longer the difference between liturgy and devotion, but the question of how spiritual exercises—individual as well as collective ones—and other genuine expressions of Christian worship can be reconnected so that the *spiritus liturgicus* about which *Sacrosanctum Concilium* speaks might continue to infuse all the segments of the people of God and their variegated occupations.

The propensity to understand what liturgy is through normative descriptions and other attempts at conceptual adequacy is related to a certain scope and focus that has long dominated theology, especially in the West and particularly at universities. To be sure, there is nothing wrong with endeavors to clarify and analyze, and darkness and opacity obviously need to make

26. An exemplary description of the liturgy in accordance with these presumptions can be found in the renowned handbook, *The Church at Prayer—Volume I: Principles of the Liturgy*, ed. Aimé-Georges Martimort, et al. (Collegeville, MN: Liturgical Press, 1987).

room for transparency and illumination everywhere, but one should not forget the narrow-mindedness of an intellectual culture which has systematically preferred cognition over other human faculties in its pursuit of truth and comprehension. When it comes to grasping the mystery that drives the liturgy and the liturgy that embodies the mystery,[27] it is important that passions, desires, impressions, emotions, and—above all else—the imagination play a prominent role as well.

It may not be an exaggeration to assert that the West has suffered from a certain *epistemologism*, which is the tendency to systematically yield the priority to knowledge and to the justification of the standards and the criteria according to which it is acquired and applied. Epistemologies and speculations about *Letztbegründung* are well and good, but only if they do not stand as a detriment to sapiential and experiential accounts of understanding. The complexity of the topics theologians deal with requires that one ultimately overcome such binary oppositions, for one will never sense the profound interwovenness God, the world, culture, and the human being unless deductions and conclusions are embedded in a broad field where wisdom and experience, tradition and community, *Vernunft* and the *Einbildungskraft* have an equal share.

In this sense, one could justifiably say that the greatest problem with modernity and secularism is not a crisis of belief in God, as if such belief were simply one opinion among a myriad of other possible convictions. To believe in God is not so much to have an explanatory idea about things but to be willing and prepared to live an exploratory life. So, rather, the greatest problem with secularism and (post-)modern cultures is indifferentism

27. For a more thorough discussion of this dynamic, see chapter 5 and also my ponderings in "Meandering in Mystery: Why Theology Today Would Benefit from Rediscovering the Work of Dom Odo Casel," in Joris Geldhof, ed., *Mediating Mysteries, Understanding Liturgies: On Bridging the Gap Between Liturgy and Systematic Theology* (Leuven: Peeters, 2015), 11–32.

and the underlying mentality that appears to be tolerant and pluralist but which ultimately blurs and devalues difference. One does not know anymore which attitude to take on *coram Deo*, or how to behave in the overwhelmingly various presence of God: the possibility that there can be something like real presence no longer makes or marks a difference. In this sense, one must agree with Charles Taylor, then, when he lucidly observes that, "in Western modernity the obstacles to belief are primarily moral and spiritual, rather than epistemic."[28] It is my conviction that the liturgy is the key, not to solve the problem, but to make sure that the access to mystery is continuously offered, "always and everywhere."

Instead of an "epistemologistic" approach to liturgy, I additionally think that a *soteriological* one is much more productive: one that takes its point of departure in the communication of the saving mysteries of the Lord, and, in so doing, immediately engages both the immanent and the economic Trinity, doxology,[29] and sacramentality. *Where is the liturgy?* The liturgy is everywhere the mystery of redemption is actualized, enacted, offered, performed, transmitted, implemented. It is wherever assemblies gather to praise the Lord in communion with the angels and the saints and in accordance with the apostolic witness. *When is the liturgy?* The liturgy is any time the church is doing what she is supposed to do, that is, when she works through her "agenda" and when she listens to and speaks the Word of God. The liturgy is when the Body of Christ is sacramentally seen and ecclesially realized,[30] and when the people of God actually become what they are supposed to be: "a chosen race, a royal priesthood, a holy nation, God's own people"

28. Taylor, "A Catholic Modernity?," 177.

29. Geoffrey Wainwright, *Doxology: The Praise of God in Worship, Doctrine and Life: A Systematic Theology* (London: Epworth, 1980).

30. See in this context a famous expression from *Sermo 272* of St. Augustine: *estote quod videtis, et accipite quod estis.*

(1 Pet 2:9). Liturgy is when and where the grand transformative dynamics of being are taking place concretely (not abstractly), and when and where the traces of God's omnipresence become events of grace. Liturgy is when and where, at the crossroads of *anabasis* and *katabasis*, the paschal mystery, in its full or partial glory, including the entire history of salvation, becomes accessible for human bodies and their senses.[31]

It is evident that such a topography and chronography of liturgy cannot be easily encapsulated within the schemas and confines of an objectifying logic. This approach may additionally be puzzling for minds that can only function with empirical exactitude, methodological rigidity, and absolute notional certainty. One can easily imagine hundreds of instances where there is a grey zone and where it is not so clear whether or not a practice, a posture, an expression, a gesture, a prayer, an assembly, or an experience is liturgy. But this is precisely the point: liturgy escapes yes-or-no questions. It is much more interesting and fruitful to ask *how much* liturgy there is in all these and many other instances. In other words, liturgy is best understood in terms of ecclesial and sacramental density.[32] Through a fascinating variety and an ingenious mutual entangledness of *legomena* and *drômena* (and *sigè*, not to forget) the church communicates the very mysteries to which she owes her own existence, outlook, energy, and stability, and ensures the possibility for humanity to "actively," "fully," and "consciously" participate in them.

It is important to stress that the proposed topographical (c.q. chronographical) approach does not, and should not, give rise

---

31. See also Catherine Pickstock, "Sense and Sacrament," in *The Oxford Handbook of Sacramental Theology*, ed. Hans Boersma and Mathew Levering (Oxford: Oxford University Press, 2015), 657–74.

32. Initial inspiration for such an approach could be drawn from Louis-Marie Chauvet, *Le corps, chemin de Dieu. Les sacrements* (Paris: Bayard, 2010), 35–54, where he elaborates some examples.

to any kind of relativism. It does relate (to) everything and is after relations and relatedness. And that is precisely the opposite of a relativistic attitude, which cuts off things and no longer puts them into the right perspective (orthodoxy). A topography of liturgy, which lays bare moments of ecclesio-sacramental density continues to subscribe to an understanding of Christian worship according to a traditional triple threefold of registers: the one of the Eucharist, the sacraments and the Liturgy of the Hours; the one of the daily, weekly, and yearly cycles of the liturgical year; and the one of the universal church, the local church, and the household or domestic church. The universal economy of salvation is operative through all of them, simultaneously, everywhere and always. Liturgical theologians are invited to explain how this magnificent *opus Dei* works. It is a universal transformative dynamics of which the Lord is the hinge.

A Universal Transformative Dynamics

In other words, Jesus Christ, the Son of God and Savior of humankind, establishes a universal extension of God's grace, which, as a gift to the church, his bride, can be distributed everywhere. This gift, however, is not something that can be stocked; it is like the manna in the desert, good food for the journey. This nourishment is the essential energy for the intrinsic liturgico-sacramental potential of changing everything in every culture, so that the world, secular or not, adapts itself increasingly to the vision of the kingdom. Aidan Kavanagh specifies:

> He [the God-Man] does not transform culture as such. He recreates the World not by making new things but by making all things new. He does this by divine power working upon all that is through the agency of a human nature he holds in solidarity with us. He summons all into a restored communion with his Father, not in spite of matter but through matter, even spit and dirt, thereby

clarifying the true meaning of the material world itself. He summons all to his Father in time, thereby renewing both time and its spatial functions. He addresses all people not only in mind and soul but in body as well, thereby renewing the human person in his and her relation to matter, to time and space, and to the whole created world.[33]

This peculiar way in which the mystery of salvation is crocheted into the universe—moreover, in such a way that the threads orient one towards the ultimate fulfillment—needs some further refinement. The universal transformative dynamics of the sanctifying mystery, as it is embodied in the liturgy of the church, allows one to look at common differences and oppositions *differently*. For the sake of brevity, I will only develop four antagonisms which should not be that. Both their agony and their being "anti" can and should be transformed, or liberated or renewed, when they are touched by "the Body of Christ."

a) Church and world. The relation between church and world is always a complex and multifaceted one, and secularism makes no fundamental difference in this respect. The church is in the world with the vocation of making it into a better place to live. Inasmuch as secularist ideologies are obstacles to that vocation, critical discernment is obviously needed. However, inasmuch as secularist ideas are harmless or, maybe paradoxically, inasmuch as they provide a stimulating environment for the flourishing of the gospel and the communities living from it, the partnership with their proponents needs to be continuously researched and evaluated as well. A continuous dialogue is not an option; it is a necessity.

In this context, Aidan Kavanagh has come up with a healthy, disarming hermeneutical key which is based in the conviction

33. Kavanagh, *On Liturgical Theology*, 50.

that secularism may not—or at least may not *always*—be equated with worldliness. The consequence of secularism, Kavanagh contends, may be that one is not worldly enough, or in other words, that it is possible to become too radically detached or alienated from engagement in the world and from care for its inhabitants. According to Kavanagh, secularism runs the risk of producing

> people who are awash in an oceanic ideology of shifting intimacy which is replete with uncontrolled, unanchored, and undirected sacralities. It is unworldly to the point of being creepy, for what it amounts to is the effacement of the *res publica* by the preference to believe that social meanings are generated only by the feelings of individual human beings.[34]

In particular, if secularism goes hand-in-hand with a libertarian view on human autonomy, with an idealization of the bonds between science, technology, and the manipulation of creation, as well as with an economic paradigm of endless commercial commodification, then it may be in dire need of a liturgical corrective to regain its concrete footing in the earth. There are contexts in which not secularism but the church and her official worship preserve the connection of humankind with the cosmos. We need thinkers who can make this point convincingly and in all kinds of fora, well aware that a persuasive strategy based on the assumption that "I am right and the others are wrong" will not only prove ineffective but will also, necessarily stand opposed to liturgical and human wisdom.

b) Heaven and earth. Whether it was unwilling or unable, it was modern cosmology that ceased to see the intricacies of the interaction between heaven and earth, and because of its being impregnated by epistemologism, it drew sharp dividing lines

---

34. Kavanagh, *On Liturgical Theology*, 28.

rather than connections. At the same time, to the extent that images of heaven and hell were historically used to superintend masses of people so that a select elite might shamelessly profit from this culture of culpability, what was said and believed about heaven *demanded* the critical treatment enabled by secularism. However, as is so often the case, the baby went out with the bathwater, and it was no longer possible to talk about heaven at all.

Nevertheless, from a soteriological and sacramental point of view, heaven is where the choirs of the angels sing and, as we on earth celebrate the liturgy, we join in their eternal song of praise and glory. That is not only a comforting thought or image but also an ecclesial action that bears a symbolic meaning of the utmost importance. It is constitutive of the church's eternal call to divine worship and, as such, of the necessarily doxological dimension of liturgy. In his thoughtful reflections about a new liturgical culture, Cardinal Kasper rightly notes: "Die Liturgie ist Gottesverehrung ('cultus divinus') oder sie ist nicht mehr Liturgie."[35] Liturgy is worship of God or it is no longer liturgy.

Furthermore, in his groundbreaking reflections on the church's "true piety," aptly translated by Virgil Michel as *Liturgy the Life of the Church*, Dom Lambert Beauduin recalls: "Between the Church of heaven and the Church of the earth there exists an intimate union which shall one day become perfect."[36] One could consider the liturgy as the motor towards that perfection. A secularist ideology is actually not able to shut down that motor. It may make it difficult to drive the car, but the

---

35. Walter Kasper, *Aspekte einer Theologie der Liturgie: Liturgie angesichts der Krise der Moderne—für eine neue liturgische Kultur*, in *Die Liturgie der Kirche*, Gesammelte Schriften, Bd. 10 (Freiburg—Basel—Wien: Herder, 2012), 42.

36. Lambert Beauduin, *Liturgy the Life of the Church*, trans. Virgil Michel (Collegeville, MN: Liturgical Press, 1929), 22.

engine will run as long as the economy of salvation provides the fuel.

c) Cult and culture. Cult and culture have the same etymological origin, and there is some evidence that they also came into being simultaneously. However, the Christian cult can never coincide with any specific culture. Charles Taylor is very firm on this and I think he is right: "There can never be a total fusion of the faith and any particular society, and the attempt to achieve it is dangerous for the faith."[37] From a historical perspective, it is definitely true that we are still trying to come to terms with the effects of the Christendom, "the attempt to marry the faith with a form of culture and a mode of society,"[38] which was moreover transplanted into many other cultural environments.

The Christian liturgy may again assist in developing a better balance between faith and culture. Through the grand vision it maintains, it may help undermine secular ideologies—from nationalism, ethnocentrism, populism, racism, libertarianism, anti-Semitism, ageism, sexism, communism, homophobia, and xenophobia to the many illusions that we can create and manage absolute security with military means and an increase of police powers. The liturgy should play in full its desacralizing role vis-à-vis the many taboos and utopias of contemporary culture. And then it can calmly propose its *heterotopia* and *heterochronia*: a world of cult, prayer, rite, and worship that actually and actively participates in Christ's salvific work and thereby anticipates humanity's divinization.

It will require considerable and concerted effort to show that this is about much more than adding (again) a bit of spirituality in a materialist culture. One must avoid any tendency to fall back into Manichaean representations of reality and

---

37. Taylor, "A Catholic Modernity?," 170.
38. Taylor, "A Catholic Modernity?," 170.

realize that there is indeed an intrinsic threat of a "gnostic return in modernity"[39] and, for that matter, also in Christianity. Liturgy itself, however, offers an intelligent alternative way of dealing with matter, for it is precisely through materiality and corporeality that our salvation has been achieved. The famous French theologian Louis-Marie Chauvet lucidly says:

> According to Church tradition, the most "spiritual" communication of God (that of the Holy Spirit itself), and thus the truth of the believing subject, takes place through this language, eminently sensory and bodily. The sacraments accordingly teach us that *the truest things in our faith occur in no other way than through the concreteness of the "body."*[40]

Or, as he puts it elsewhere in a more concise manner, "*the most "spiritual" happens through the most "corporeal."*"[41]

In addition, I think that a renewed sensitivity for symbols is at stake. The mediations of cult and culture cannot be beneficial for Christian liturgy *or* for secular culture unless a symbolic conversion takes place, that is, a shift from semiotics to an ontology of language, or, from sign and signification theories to a metaphysics of symbolicity. In this respect, I once again side with Louis Dupré, who holds that "Without an innate capacity to reach out to what lies beyond itself the religious mind would be incapable of receiving, understanding, and much less of articulating a transcendent message."[42] This unreservedly applies to liturgy in cultures of the present day. Dupré also maintains: "A truly symbolic relation must be

39. Cyril O'Regan, *Gnostic Return in Modernity* (Albany, NY: State University of New York Press, 2001).

40. Louis-Marie Chauvet, *Symbol and Sacrament: A Sacramental Reinterpretation of Christian Existence* (Collegeville, MN: Liturgical Press, 1995), 140–41.

41. Chauvet, *Symbol and Sacrament*, 146.

42. Dupré, *Symbols of the Sacred*, 125.

grounded in Being itself. Nothing exposes our religious impoverishment more directly than the loss of the ontological dimension of language."[43] Again, this insight unreservedly applies to our topic: liturgy is exactly the place where culture can learn (again) a capacity for symbols, and as a corollary, a receptivity for transcendence.

d) Religion and politics. At an institutional level, it is best that state and church make practical arrangements so that the one does not directly interfere with the daily business and the infrastructure of the other, but this does not imply that either need undertake exceptional efforts to prevent religion and politics from interacting. Even where such efforts are pursued, religion and politics will always come into contact, whether the most committed defenders of *laïcité* like it or not. Moreover, if it is true, as Alexander Schmemann famously suggested, that the church, her "orthodoxy" and her sacraments are there "for the life of the world,"[44] then it follows that the liturgy has severe political consequences.

Foremost among these consequences, and as any reflection about or experience of the liturgy must attest, liturgy leaves no room for the radical or liberal individualism of the day. Beauduin decidedly contends:

> From the very first centuries to our own day, the Church has ever given to all her prayer a character profoundly and essentially collective. By means of living the liturgy wholeheartedly, Christians become more and more conscious of their supernatural fraternity, of their union in the mystic body of Christ.[45]

---

43. Dupré, *Religion and the Rise*, 116.
44. Alexander Schmemann, *For the Life of the World: Sacraments and Orthodoxy* (Crestwood, NY: St Vladimir's Seminary Press, 1973).
45. Beauduin, *Liturgy the Life of the Church*, 23–24.

Liturgy does not tolerate the whimsical preferences and alleg-edly free choices of the individual as the highest criterion for the organization, neither of itself nor of society. Rather, it sup-poses and promotes deeply human and personal qualities which give evidence of veritable solidarity, connectedness, and empathy. Romano Guardini expounds:

> The requirements of the liturgy can be summed up in one word, humility. Humility by renunciation; that is to say, by the abdication of self-rule and self-sufficiency. And humility by positive action; that is to say, by the accep-tance of the spiritual principles which the liturgy offers and which far transcend the little world of individual spiritual existence.[46]

Second, whatever initiative Christians take or support in the public arena must be guided by catholicity and apostolicity. This does not mean that the prerogatives of the Catholic Church must be defended against all odds, but that the things the apostles received and passed on continue to work posi-tively for people throughout the world (*kath'holon*). Kavanagh sketches the contours of this "agenda" in his typical prose as follows:

> The World sets the City's agenda, an agenda which is then executed in the City's workshop, the Church. The scope of this agenda is such that the Church must first of all be and act in a manner which is catholic, that is, City-wide and Worldwide in its nature and ends. Catholicity is a quality endowed upon Church by City and World. It is not a quality which the Church generates for itself, in its own self-interest according to criteria which are the Church's own. . . . The Church and sectarianism are thus

---

46. Romano Guardini, *The Spirit of the Liturgy*, Milestones in Catholic Theology (New York: Crossroad, 1998), 39.

antithetical entities, and that the Church Catholic is one
denomination among others, a sort of religious boutique
in the suburbs, is an unthinkable proposition. When the
Church fails at being catholic, it begins to fail at being
one, holy, and apostolic as well.[47]

Concluding Observation

Much of the theoretical groundwork for the rest this book
have been laid out in this chapter. We have looked at the history of ideas and at the present situation, from which we can
draw a double conclusion: first, that liturgy and secularism
are not extreme opposites, and second, that a more nuanced
and detailed process of discernment is needed to study and
comment upon the ways in which they interact.

---

47. Kavanagh, *On Liturgical Theology*, 43.

CHAPTER 2

Liturgy, Ideology and Politics

A very important characteristic of modernity to which allusions were made in the previous chapter is the emergence of ideologies. This is to say that attempts to establish control over reality have historically coincided with strong sets of ideas about how to organize and maintain that control successfully. Modernity is not only concerned with the subject's autonomy or with vouchsafing methods of scientific and rational reasoning as the sole warrants for truth; it is also preoccupied with the vision, and indeed the promise, of the universal realizability of projects. Many interpretations of modernity stress that the radically new understanding of science developed between the sixteenth and seventeenth centuries was progressively combined with technological and economic developments previously unthought-of. Modernity, however, had its roots in a fundamental shift in the way human beings interact with—and understand—the reality surrounding them. It is because of this shift that the changes in science, politics, religion, society, and culture could arise, not vice versa.[1] In the political realm, modernity saw the

---

1. This argumentation is developed at large in the work of authors like Hans Blumenberg, Charles Taylor, and Louis Dupré. Within the scope of this book it is not necessary to discuss these theories in detail.

establishment of nation-states and the corresponding emergence of bureaucracies.[2]

This evolution brought about the proceduralization of exchange, both between citizens and the state as well as between citizens among themselves. These citizens increasingly functionalized the world and their relationships, as they became employers or employees and producers or consumers in many different areas of life. Moreover, these roles went also far beyond labor and commerce, as they equally affected health, education, mobility, leisure, etc. As will be discussed in more detail below, an ideology can be understood as the fruit of the reflection about strategies to manage all of these manifold interactions in the most efficient way. However, in addition to that reflection (which is never neutral, of course) ideologies contain and employ mechanisms of persuasion which naturally deny or sidetrack alternatives to their own proposals and ideas. Since they are fundamentally directed towards dominion, they lose a sense of openness and a sensitivity for the complexity of reality.

Inasmuch as modernity does not take anything for granted and supposes that everything (can and) must be created by the self,[3] modernity and the emergence of ideologies are necessarily intertwined. Ideologies design the programs of the modern self. Those programs actually originate in a deep mistrust towards being, "for 'modern' has always meant: that for which nothing is given, not even itself."[4] At the same time, if

---

2. Interestingly, the emergence of modern bureaucracies seems to have preceded the development of democracies. Generally, modern democracies have kept modern bureaucracies in order to keep the system going. It seems not possible to have democracy without bureaucracy.

3. Fundamental in this respect is Charles Taylor, *Sources of the Self: The Making of the Modern Identity* (Cambridge, MA: Harvard University Press, 1989).

4. Jean-Luc Nancy, *Adoration: The Deconstruction of Christianity II*, trans. John McKeane (New York: Fordham University Press, 2013), 45.

it is true that liturgy can only be understood from a sense of givenness, there cannot but be a fundamental tension between modernity and liturgy.

In line with what has been said already in the previous chapter, the present one tries to catch this tension and its multiple variants. It seeks an answer to a whole complex of interrelated questions: What is actually meant by secularization? Is it only about a variation of the ancient opposition between old and new? What is the relation between modernity and secularization? Where does the tenacious but often unuttered idea originate that worship and modernity are mutually exclusive? Are modernity and secularization at fault for the fact that Christian worship has been receding from public life, at least in Western Europe? Or is it the other way around: is the church guilty of this development because it failed to sufficiently adapt its liturgical actions and language to modern and secular culture? Or is secularization about a paradoxical interplay of two mutually reinforcing tendencies? How could the Christian liturgy escape secularization? Must it even attempt to escape it? Is secularization a threat or an opportunity? Can liturgy be more or less secular, and is one of these possibilities a good and the other a bad thing? Is it helpful to suggest that the liturgy is a phenomenon to be situated outside of the secular and anti-secular ideologies?

In order to somehow address this vast range of questions, this chapter is divided into four parts. In the first, I want to introduce two different interpretations of modernity from a solely historical perspective. These two perspectives quite obviously impel the debate about the relation between liturgy and secularization into opposite directions. I secondly attempt to philosophically deepen the insights gained into the nature of modernity and of secularization by discussing central aspects of the theories of philosophers Louis Dupré and Charles Taylor, who figured already in the previous chapter. While these thinkers largely neglect the practical side of (the

Christian) religion as cult and worship in a manner typical of the intellectual development of the West, I will focus precisely on the consequences of their perspectives for the liturgy. In the third section, I show how ideologization and politicization are inherently connected to secularization and modernity. This connection poses a particular challenge to the liturgy. For precisely insofar as the liturgy falls prey to the pressure of secularization, it is no different than an ordinary political phenomenon and problem. The question, then, is whether and to what extent liturgy can still maintain its theological particularity. This question is the subject of the fourth and last part of this chapter. I conclude with an unambiguous suggestion as to what course the liturgy might take in modernity.

1. Two Interpretations of Modernity

One frequently hears that it was not until the Second Vatican Council that the Catholic Church began to open its doors to modernity. There is disagreement about whether or not this was too late (only very few think it was too early), but there at least seems to be consensus around the assessment itself. But what is meant by this opening to modernity?

It is certain that some developments stemming from Vatican II were generally judged to be positive: the turn towards the contemporary world in all its complexity, the departure from a style of condemning all that is "other," the overcoming of fears of various intellectual systems and societal tendencies as well as the church's acceptance of "the human" in general, of the *humanum*. Much of this is connected to the fact that the council consciously understood itself as "pastoral" and, in this manner, aligned itself with the future-oriented vision of John XXIII.[5] The

---

5. Ephrem Carr, "*Sacrosanctum concilium* and its Consequences: The Reform of the Liturgy," *Questions Liturgiques/Studies in Liturgy* 92 (2011): 183–94.

constitution *Gaudium et Spes* is especially viewed as a singular event in the continual development of the relation between the church and the modern world. *Sacrosanctum Concilium*, too, is much appreciated because it implemented necessary adjustments intended to bring the liturgy closer to contemporary men and women.[6] The reform of the liturgy generally counts as a successful project of the global church's efforts to bring itself into better accordance with the requirements and preconditions of the modern world.

The question, however, is whether the understanding of modernity underlying this viewpoint is in fact adequate. In a historic study of the Council of Trent, Wolfgang Reinhard distinguishes between "relative" and "absolute" modernity. On the one hand, modernity can be understood as an irrevocable historical development that can be characterized according to different, mutually reinforcing elements: the emancipation of the individual from traditional, institutional, structural as well as moral authorities located above or beyond its limits and reach, and that it cannot therefore control or modify, let alone approve. Modernity awakens the awareness that these authorities cannot probably (fully) justify themselves (for much longer) and, for this reason, suggests alternative discourses of liberation from them. In this case, Reinhard calls modernity "relative." On the other hand, modernity can also be understood as the human being's specific and complex interaction with his or her environment—an interaction characterized by the attempt to determine natural processes and to organize this domination as efficiently as possible. However, this

6. See, e.g., Rita Ferrone, *Liturgy:* Sacrosanctum Concilium: *Rediscovering Vatican II* (New York: Paulist Press, 2007; Kevin W. Irwin, *What We Have Done, What We Have Failed to Do: Assessing the Liturgical Reforms of Vatican II* (New York: Paulist Press, 2013); Carmel Pilcher, David Orr, and Elizabeth Harrington, eds., *Vatican Council II: Reforming Liturgy* (Adelaide: ATF Theology, 2013).

approach inevitably leads to a diversification of functions, to a very particular type of rationalization and to disciplining. Reinhard calls modernity thus understood "absolute."[7]

Reinhard describes not merely two interpretations of modernity but also claims that the absolute form (*Gestalt*) is much more persistent than the relative form. Before the Second World War, the church was certainly not modern in the "relative" sense. According to a widespread opinion, it is indeed only since the 1960s that the image of open doors and windows applies. In view of an evaluation of the pontificates of Paul VI, John Paul II, and Benedict XVI, many also ask whether this openness was merely a historically contingent and contextual matter rather than a structural adjustment and a definite achievement. In contrast, it is clear for Reinhard that the church has already been modern in an absolute sense—and acted accordingly—since the sixteenth century. The general conduct and self-organization of the Catholic Church is not significantly different or distinguishable from another typical product of

---

7. Wolfgang Reinhard, "Il concilio di Trento e la modernizzazione della Chiesa. Introduzione," in *Il concilio di Trento e il moderno*, Annali dell'Istituto storico italo-germanico 45, ed. P. Prodi and Wolfgang Reinhard (Bologna: Il Mulino, 1996), 27–53. One may justifiably doubt whether Reinhard's terminology is the best one possible. This is probably not the case, for the concepts "relative" and "absolute" evoke too many philosophical complexities. Nevertheless, I will not hazard alternatives to Reinhard's terms because I think that they have a not unimportant advantage, too. Reinhard cleverly avoids the notions of premodern, postmodern, late-modern, and the like. Although he doesn't explicitly reflect on that choice, I see it as an interesting move that he interprets "modernity" not exclusively, or primarily, as an identifiable historical period. Rather, modernity is a paradigmatic concept, which helps one come to terms with (interpretations of) modernity and modernization in a philosophical way, i.e., without bothering too much about historical questions about when and where it began and (whether it had already) ended. The truth may be that, even if we are already in a so-called (post-)postmodern situation, there is still a great amount of modernity among, around, and within us.

the modern era, the nation-state. The church and modern states largely operate bureaucratically, erect comprehensive administrations for all their procedures and operations, organize themselves hierarchically, and appeal to the law in all things.

It is not unimportant to ask what this perspective might imply for the phenomenon of the liturgy. It is clear for many that if the Council of Trent did not initiate an absolute-modern mentality with regard to the liturgy, it at the very least confirmed, enforced, and handed down such a mentality. The liturgy became a comprehensive legal system with clear prescriptions and rules, functionaries who regulated and controlled their administration, schools that prepared these functionaries for their commissions, and so on. Perhaps commentators like Giuseppe Alberigo and James White are correct in suggesting that for the history of the liturgy after Trent, the establishment of the Sacred Congregation of Rites in 1588 has been more important than the content of the *Missale Romanum*.[8]

It seems difficult to judge whether and how far this absolute-modern mentality in the realm of the liturgy was brought to a halt with the promulgation of the Constitution on the Sacred Liturgy, *Sacrosanctum Concilium,* in 1963 and whether it was definitively superseded by a relative modernity. I am disinclined to negate this *tout court*; and yet it is very probable that relative and absolute modernity do not relate to one another absolutely but relatively and that it is not therefore one *or* the other which exists, but always different quantities of both. I now want to show how this is possible by way of a cultural-philosophical excursus.

2. Modernity, Secularization and Liturgy

Secularization and modernity are inherently connected. Although Christianity has always known conflicts between

8. See chapter 1.

political and religious authorities, in the modern age, the tension between the faith on the one hand and culture and society on the other takes on a wholly new form. The modern and the secular can be interpreted and evaluated in different ways, however. With a view to what concerns us here, the liturgy, it seems useful to highlight several points.

1. Firstly, modernity should not be confused or identified with any one of its particular forms (*Gestalten*). One often finds theologians, as well as other scholars of the humanities, simply equating modernity and the Enlightenment. If one takes a closer look at their theories and critique, one notices that they in fact merely point to the boundaries of scientific rationality and that they identify the uncompromising defense of this particular manner of acquiring knowledge with the Enlightenment. Of course this is much too simplistic. The Enlightenment is a much more comprehensive phenomenon; it cannot be traced back to some rationalism, empiricism, or scientific positivism. The Enlightenment is of course much more than the advancement of a particular epistemology. More importantly, however, the Enlightenment must not at all be equated with modernity.

In this context, the American philosopher of culture Louis Dupré has come up with a highly useful metaphor. He speaks of consecutive "waves of modernity." New and unique shapes keep emerging from the water of one and the same ocean, which then lap the shores of humanity.

According to Dupré, modernity emerged in the context of intellectual developments during the late Middle Ages and, in various phases, has asserted itself until today. These waves or phases are that of the Renaissance and of humanism, of the Enlightenment and the Romantic era, which are all "modern," yet which cannot simply be reduced to a common denominator.[9] No one phase is the cause or preparation for the next, but

9. Louis Dupré, *Religion and the Rise of Modern Culture* (Notre Dame: Notre Dame University Press, 2008), 29: "The three stages of modern

at most a precondition.[10] Postmodernity may not be the result of modernity and the birth of a decisively new socio-cultural reality but merely a fourth wave from the same modern sea.

Thus, if we suspect tensions to exist between modernity and liturgy, it will not do to make a plea for idiosyncratic symbolic universes like the Christian liturgy, and as a consequence, to view, implicitly or explicitly, scientific rationality as one's opponent. Such a strategy seems too superficial and naïve. Instead, one must think more deeply about the scope and significance of modernity and secularization.

2. As is widely known, Charles Taylor has engaged with the phenomenon of secularism and secularization in considerable depth.[11] His insight that secularization in the modern sense has primarily to do with separation seems especially pertinent. Originally the *saeculum* referred to profane time and was therefore distinguished from eternal time. At least since the Reformation and the seventeenth century, the meaning of the word has shifted. The spread of the term's usage and its conceptual enlargement of a simple indication of time to a much broader category also brought with it a radicalization. The new understanding "affirms, in effect, that the 'lower'—immanent or secular—order is all that there is and that the higher—or

---

culture—humanism and the Renaissance, the Enlightenment, and the period following the French Revolution—shared some basic principles. Yet their relation was never one in which the earlier stage 'caused' the later one. Each presented a creative event in its own right, even though the later could not have emerged without the earlier. Nor can the periods be reduced to a common denominator. Each expressed a different innovative impulse, yet together they constituted a single cultural epoch."

10. I will come back more extensively to this waves theory of modernity in chapter 3.

11. For a solid introduction and interesting comments, see James K. A. Smith, *How (Not) To Be Secular: Reading Charles Taylor* (Grand Rapids, MI: Eerdmans, 2014).

transcendent—is a human invention."[12] In other words, the distinction led to a divorce—and the divorce to a dismissal of one of the two truncated parts.

This separation and the dismissal of the other-than-secular or transcendent has consequences for religion that are impossible to overlook. For according to the possible etymologies of the word, "religion," represents a reality that "connects" and "holds together." In the introduction to his magnum opus *A Secular Age*, published in 2007, Taylor distinguishes between three dimensions of religion's relation to the "beyond": (1) "The sense that there is some good higher than, beyond human flourishing," (2) "a possibility of transformation . . . which takes us beyond merely human perfection," and (3) the demand that "we see our life as going beyond the bounds of its 'natural' scope between birth and death."[13] Religion holds these three dimensions of transcendence together. It is therefore more than a system of transcendent truths—it is a phenomenon relevant to life in all its aspects.

What was just said about religion in general is especially true for the liturgy. If secularization makes it impossible to feel the transcendent in the immanent because the intertwining of the eternal and the temporal is viewed and dismissed as merely a human illusion, then the liturgy is simply done for.

This is why I sometimes think that the twenty-first century should become the century of the heavenly liturgy, as the twentieth century was that of active participation. We have to rediscover the notion that active participation exists not merely among ourselves but also between us and heaven—that is, that we can actively participate in the heavenly realm. When *Sacrosanctum Concilium* claims that "in the earthly liturgy we take

12. Taylor, "What Does Secularism Mean?," in *Dilemmas and Connections: Selected Essays* (Cambridge, MA: The Belknap Press of Harvard University Press, 2011), 305.

13. Charles Taylor, *A Secular Age* (Cambridge, MA: The Belknap Press of Harvard University Press, 2007), 20.

part in a foretaste of that heavenly liturgy which is celebrated in the holy city of Jerusalem toward which we journey as pilgrims," and that "with all the hosts of heaven we sing a hymn of glory to the Lord" and that, in "venerating the memory of the saints, we hope to share their company,"[14] then there definitely exists an irresolvable tension with the most radical forms of secularization as defined by Taylor. If the separation between the earthly and the heavenly realm is absolutized, then the liturgy is dead. For in a precise and substantial sense, the liturgy is God's work (*opus Dei*) and at the same time the work of His people (the *ergon* of the *laos*).

3. Let us go a step further in the exploration of modernity and its relation to religion and faith. What would be modernity's fundamental attitude towards religion(s) and towards human religiosity?

Both Taylor and Dupré seem to suggest that what is at issue is not a conflict over knowledge. Faith is ultimately not about a kind of knowledge that would contrast or fight with scientific knowledge. The many epistemological debates about the existence of God and the certainty of faith claims have thus reached a certain limit. Charles Taylor knows about a deeper level that extends beyond the "mainline Enlightenment story," according to which religion loses credibility the further the triad of science, technology, and economics progresses. Taylor is convinced that the "main story" has to do with moral and existential factors rather than with quarrels over the adequacy of knowledge and epistemic certainty.

Louis Dupré makes a similar claim in denying the prominent position and preeminent role of reason or the mind in modern rationalism as its most fundamental problem: "The root of the rationalist problem consists not in the creation of a false universalism, not in the exclusive reliance on a priori methods of reasoning, but in the attribution of the sources of

---

14. *Sacrosanctum Concilium* 8.

reason exclusively to the human mind."[15] What is most important, therefore, is that, in the entirety of reality, the modern
subject has become a lonely creature because it can no longer
really hear anything but itself.

This critical analysis is of course highly problematic for the
liturgy. For by its very nature the liturgy is corporal and draws
its life from another distinct from itself; it even maintains a
dialogical, that is, not merely a dialectical, relation with this
radical alterity. The liturgy involves not only talk *about* but also
with God. God speaks through the liturgy.

Neither Taylor nor Dupré is convinced that one need reject
modernity in order to once more make space for religion. According to Taylor, secularization has created new cultural,
intellectual, ethical, and social conditions.[16] These conditions
certainly do not make the continued existence of religion and
faith impossible. Moreover, to ignore or to fight these new
frameworks are not viable options. Dupré reminds us that
modernity in its enlightened form exercised a definite influence
on Christianity. Religious tolerance, the separation of church
and state, respect for individual conscience, the repudiation
of political coercion, social pressure, and cultural prejudices
have become nonnegotiable items of the Western mentality,
no less among those who are religious. Additionally, historical
criticism of biblical texts has forced the church to adjust its
occasionally blind literalness. This was often an embarrassing
matter, especially where the critique was articulated sarcasti-
cally. Yet Dupré is of the opinion that these modern developments were ultimately more of a blessing than a curse.[17]

I think that something similar applies in the realm of the
liturgy. It is still possible to celebrate the Christian mysteries of
the faith, even if modernity and secularization have created a

---

15. Dupré, *Religion and the Rise*, 39.
16. This aspect is particularly important for Smith, *How (Not) To Be Secular*.
17. Dupré, *Religion and the Rise*, 40.

world entirely different from that in which the liturgy emerged. The solution cannot lie in trying to resurrect the old world or in assuming it to be possible—or necessary—to somehow keep this alive. The cult must always be distinguished from culture, irrespective of the latter's typological qualification, historical context, geographical distribution, or its societal success. In this context, Taylor proposes a distinction between Christianity (or the Christian faith) and Christendom, arguing (from a distinctly normative perspective) that, if the faith and church coincide in totality with culture and custom, this is never beneficial for the faith.[18] I think this is true and important. It also implies that the liturgy cannot be determined or defined by ideologies.

3. Liturgy and Ideology

Yet there is a great risk that the liturgy in modern and secular contexts falls prey to ideologies. I thus want to show why this is the case and what ideologies are capable of. I then attempt to indicate how, in a modern or secular environment, ideology and politics are intertwined with one another. My goal in doing so is to explain and justify the theological opinion that, in keeping with its a-ideological nature, the liturgy can and should avoid the oppositions between "modern" versus "anti-modern," or "secular" and "anti-secular."

For a definition of ideology I appeal to the fundamental work *Ideology and Utopia* by Karl Mannheim, the first German edition of which was already published in 1929. According to Mannheim, an ideology develops out of a fundamental mistrust for one's opponents in debate—a mistrust which is founded on the assumption that such opponents operate under bogus or disingenuous sets of convictions that obscure reality and truth and which are set to lead me, too, astray. This is only the first step, however. Things only become ideological in a

18. See chapter 1.

total sense when this view of reality bypasses the psychological level and when it moreover manifests itself in the unconscious and as a key interrelational reference point. Mannheim claims that entire historical eras and complete world views can be pervaded by ideologies and, as a moral recommendation, adds that it is important not only to suspect ideological elements in the mindset of others but also to recognize one's own ideological presuppositions:

> As long as one does not call his own position into question but regards it absolute, while interpreting his opponents' ideas as a mere function of the social positions they occupy, the decisive step has not been taken. . . . In contrast to this special formulation, the general form of the total conception of ideology is being used by the analyst when he has the courage to subject not just the adversary's point of view but all points of view, including his own, to the ideological analysis.[19]

The awareness that ideologies are as comprehensive as they are subtle, and hence often almost unrecognizable, is a result of a fundamental intellectual development commonly referred to as modernity. Mannheim says that the emergence of ideologies is connected to modern epistemologies, which can only view reason and meaning as realizations of the subject—and in this he seems to be in agreement with Dupré. The loss of the objective and ontological unity of the world, which Mannheim associates with the medieval Christian worldview, was followed by a subjective unity, which was guaranteed only by the absolute subject of modernity (Mannheim here really speaks only of the Enlightenment).

---

19. Karl Mannheim, *Ideology and Utopia: An Introduction to the Sociology of Knowledge* (New York: Harcourt, Brace & Co., 1954), 68–69.

Henceforth the world as "world" exists only with reference to the knowing mind, and the mental activity of the
subject determines the form in which the world appears.
This constitutes in fact the embryonic total conception of
ideology, though it is, as yet, devoid of its historical and
sociological implications. [20]

In this context it must be pointed out that what makes the
liturgy *liturgy* is something quite practical. It is a work (*ergon*)
and it is executed. It is therefore more closely related to metal-
lurgy and surgery than to the theoretical approaches of the respective sciences, to acting than to knowledge, to performance
than to information. For the liturgy derives its identity not initially from notional contents, from the coherence between them
and from their justification in theoretical contexts. The liturgy
is poetic rather than noetic. That is why it can never really be
absorbed by any particular ideology. Concepts can never suc-
ceed at fully capturing it. No "logic" fully captures it without
destroying its "-urgical" nature. That is why one can speak of
an ontological incommensurability of liturgy and ideology. They
cannot be measured by the same yardstick; they adhere to fundamentally different principles. To introduce the liturgy as a
transparent, comprehensible content ultimately amounts to
dragging it into the conflict between warring ideologies.

When this happens, however, then liturgy has become politics, that is, something that must be "regulated" because of
different opinions and interests. Yet this is always done by
authorities who wield power, exercise force and, sooner or
later, alienate themselves from people's concrete life. One author who offers interesting critical insights on this subject is
Italian philosopher Giorgio Agamben. Yet while Agamben, as
a result of Foucault's archeological method, aims at the deconstruction of modern economics and politics, and—perhaps

20. Mannheim, *Ideology and Utopia*, 62.

somewhat surprisingly—deals with the history of the meaning of the Christian liturgy for this particular reason, I am concerned with a theological understanding of the liturgy in contemporary cultures. By seeking to capture the particularity of the Christian liturgy, which often remains unobserved by theology and philosophy as well as by the other arts and humanities, Agamben's and my paths thus run parallel for a short while—though they will soon separate again.

According to Agamben, the Christian understanding of the economy of salvation is not fundamentally different from that of modern economics and politics. It can even be regarded as their foundation. The God of the Christian faith was a radical novelty in ancient cultures: He alone regulated and governed both heaven and earth with his providence. The early Christians could therefore speak of an economy of mystery.[21] God's "governance" extended over the whole of creation and the foundation of his kingdom comprised the entire universe.

Agamben underscores the connection, in the Christian faith, between divine image and economy:

> If we do not understand the very close connection that links *oikonomia* with providence, it is not possible to measure the novelty of Christian theology with regard to pagan mythology and "theology." Christian theology is not a "story about the gods"; it is *immediately* economy and providence, that is, an activity of self-revelation, government, and care of the world. The deity articulates itself into a trinity, but this is not a "theogony" or a "mythology"; rather, it is an *oikonomia*, that is, at the same time,

21. Giorgio Agamben, *The Kingdom and the Glory: For a Theological Genealogy of Economy and Government*, trans. Lorenzo Chiesa with Matteo Mandarini (Stanford: Stanford University Press, 2011), 26, 40. See in addition the entire second chapter of the same book, "The Mystery of the Economy," 17–52.

the articulation and administration of divine life, and the government of creatures.[22]

This articulation and administration of the divine life, which is simultaneously the administration of creatures—what would it be if not the liturgy? Is liturgy therefore nothing other than the "real" or "true" Christian politics,[23] which can never be equated with some sort of participation by Christians in secular political games with their means and ends, let alone being replaceable by such participation?

Perhaps Agamben is right when he claims that the Christian liturgy, thus understood, is more about participation in the angelic worship than about concrete societal decision making processes or practical problem-solving.

> If the politicality and truth of the *ekklèsia* is defined by its participation in the angels, then men can also reach their full celestial citizenship only by imitating the angels and participating with them in the song of praise and glorification. The political vocation of man is an angelic vocation, and the angelic vocation is a vocation to the song of glory.[24]

Now participation in the eternal praise of God through the angels, together with Mary and, not least, the Son of God himself as the only high priest, can never be an objective for secular political action or modern economics. For these always lead to the alienation of the human being from themselves, because they are founded in structures that aim at domination and efficiency. These governing structures prevent human beings from leading their lives without pressure and in full freedom.

22. Agamben, *The Kingdom and the Glory*, 47.
23. See Agamben, *The Kingdom and the Glory*, 15.
24. Agamben, *The Kingdom and the Glory*, 147.

Even if Agamben probably would not say as much—I think the liturgy is a possible way of realizing this complete liberation of the human being because it participates in the divine work of salvation and because it not only symbolically illustrates but also co-executes the same. However, in this case, the nature of the liturgy would have to lie precisely beyond the political and ideological, or put differently, would have to be apolitical and a-ideological.

So there obviously is a difference here that must be respected and whose persistence can provide us with deeper insight into the relation between liturgy, faith, and theology on the one hand and modernity and secularization on the other.

4. Liturgy and Theology in Modernity

In the spring of 2009, Giorgio Agamben gave a lecture in the Notre Dame Cathedral of Paris that has been translated into English under the title of *The Church and the Kingdom.* In it, Agamben does not explicitly speak about the liturgy, though what he says is nonetheless helpful for interpreting the role of the liturgy in the life of the church and of the members of the Body of Christ. According to Agamben, it is necessary to be oriented towards the coming of the Kingdom instead of operationalizing and organizing it by means of apparatuses and systems. The sensibility for an economy of salvation within history, Agamben argues, has become so weak that it has almost disappeared. At the same time, however, economic forces are running more and more rampant and are threatening to increasingly control all dimensions of social life.

This very process amounts to a secular reversal of the original purpose of the economy of salvation. Where there should be liturgy, there appeared, instead, economics and an economization of politics, of inter-human relations and of the law.

> The complete juridification and commodification of human relations—the confusions between what we might

> believe, hope and love and that which we are obliged to
> do or not do, say or not say—are signs not only of crises
> of law and state but also, and above all, of crises of the
> Church. The reason for this is that the Church can be a
> living institution only on the condition that it maintains
> an immediate relation to its end.[25]

The life of the church thus depends on its being-perfected, not on what she does, how she functions or how much she produces but on her *arché* and her *telos*: the liturgy. Agamben poses a poignant question, namely, whether the church in its contemporary situation can rediscover its messianic vocation.

In other words, if the church does not celebrate the liturgy, it becomes obsolete. In saying this, however, one must have a precise understanding of what it means to celebrate the liturgy. The celebration of the liturgy takes place in the world and in history, but it does not coincide with the *saeculum* in the spatial or temporal sense. It is an activity of human beings in the world without being of the world—"*du monde sans en être*," as the French philosopher and Jesuit Paul Valadier, paraphrasing the gospel, fittingly describes the essence of Christian existence.[26] To continue this activity in a modernity characterized by secularization and in a variety of cultural and linguistic contexts is perhaps the biggest contemporary challenge for the church in the West. On the one hand, the church is meant to do this in a manner that allows her, *ad extra*, to avoid completely dissolving the particularity of the liturgy in modern discourses because it thinks this the best way to protect its relevance and efficiency. On the other hand it should, *ad intra*, avoid letting the liturgy become the object of, or reason for, ideological arguments between different parties. About the

25. Giorgio Agamben, *The Church and the Kingdom*, trans. Leland de la Durantaye (New York: Seagull Books, 2012), 41–42.

26. Paul Valadier, *La condition chrétienne: du monde sans en être* (Paris: Seuil, 2003).

liturgy no one is right. Nor can it be the object of debates about more or less secularization and modernity; for it is actually pointless to claim to want to secularize or modernize the liturgy. Doing so would mean reducing it to a graspable object or to a transparent and therefore manipulable system of rules.

In order for this double strategy *ad intra* and *ad extra* to have any chance of success it seems useful, at the end of this chapter, to briefly discuss two conditions for the future of the liturgy in modernity. It must, on the one hand, constitute a persuasive universe of symbols that is rooted in reality itself (i.e., not merely preserve an arbitrary system of signs) and, on the other hand, rise to the life of human beings. It is no coincidence that these are two things pointed out by Louis Dupré and Giorgio Agamben. Yet for neither of them did the theological core of the liturgy hang in the balance. For me, however, this is of primary importance.

Dupré bemoans that under the influence of modernization processes our symbol structures have been severed from a given, natural order, which led to a situation in which only the human mind determines which order must be and what its meaning is. In this way, symbolic structures in all realms of life, among them religion, have become something like small, self-contained worlds, independent of one another and without any relation to the whole. Dupré also knows that symbols, which upon closer examination are merely arbitrarily created expressions, lack existential depth.[27] Many liturgical celebra-

---

27. Louis Dupré, *Symbols of the Sacred* (Grand Rapids, MI: Eerdmans, 2000), 123: "Having detached our symbolic structures from a *given, natural order*, we alone determine what order and its meaning ought to be. Symbolic structures in all areas, including religion, now tend to turn into mini-universes, independent of each other and unrelated to the whole. What once served as beacons of meaning on our journey through life has now ceased to provide guidance. Symbols that are no more than 'expressions' created at random lack existential significance."

tions we experience in our everyday life doubtlessly already
offer such small, self-contained worlds without reference to
reality as a whole. Perhaps they are managed by a merely autonomous reason which does not actually participate in the
Mystery and which does not know itself to be received by this
Mystery. Religious symbols and—as I would add—liturgies
presuppose "that the mind itself possesses a transcendent dimension which enables it to share in the transcendence from
which it receives its revelation."[28] This implies a fundamental
receptivity that is rooted in Being itself and that precedes every
kind of symbol activity or liturgical celebration. The future of
the liturgy in modern and secular cultures is connected with
the willingness to recognize and to (once again) experience
that every truly symbolical—and therefore also every liturgical
and sacramental—relation is founded in Being itself and is
therefore also linked to the intention of leaving behind the
religious impoverishment that was coupled with the loss of
the ontological dimension of language.[29]

Agamben seeks to find a form of life that is not subverted
or disrupted by any oppressive mechanisms such as modern
ideologies and secular administrative systems. It is for this
reason that he is interested in the monastic life.[30] For our reflection here it is important that he positions the liturgy as an
intermediate figure in the tension between life and rule. In his
view there are monastic forms of life in which the opposition
between laws and rules on the one hand and the unconstrained
life on the other is removed through the liturgy. Modernity

28. Dupré, *Symbols of the Sacred*, 125.

29. See chapters 1 and 5.

30. For a discussion of this aspect, see my essay "The Figure of the
Monk as the Ideal of a Liturgical Life? Perspectives from Contemporary
Political Philosophy and Liturgical Theology," in *International Journal of
Philosophy and Theology* 77 (2016): 237–51.

was not capable of seeing the "what" and the "how" of such a form of life, let alone of valuing or promoting it.

> What is in question in the monastic rules is thus a trans- formation that seems to bear on the very way in which human action is conceived, so that one shifts from the level of practice and acting to that of form of life and liv- ing. This dis-location of ethics and politics from the sphere of action to that of form of life represents the most demanding legacy of monasticism, which modernity has failed to recognize.[31]

But perhaps this change and this shift are nothing other than the liturgy and the liturgization of life the liturgy facilitates. However, these processes can in no way be coordinated by modern-secular forms of logic.

---

31 Giorgio Agamben, *The Highest Poverty: Monastic Rules and Form-of-Life*, trans. Adam Kotsko (Stanford: Stanford University Press, 2013), 61.

CHAPTER 3

Liturgy Beyond Sacred and Profane

The central idea developed in this chapter is that the reality designated by the concept of "the sacred" on the one hand and salvation in a Christian sense on the other hand never coincide, and that the liturgy can never be adequately understood on the basis of an analysis of the sacred alone. However, it is often tempting to identify liturgy and the sacred, especially in the context of worship, for one knows that it comprises the place where Christians solemnly celebrate the fact that God has offered salvation to humankind, in particular through Jesus Christ. I move forward the hypothesis that, if one wants this (faith) conviction to be acknowledged as true, one has to found it on a clear distinction between salvation and the sacred. By saying "distinction," however, I don't imply a "separation." For, as a matter of fact, one can do two things in the case of a conceptual tension. One can either accentuate the intrinsic connection between the two poles or one can emphasize the difference. With respect to salvation and the sacred, it seems opportune to put forward the difference, because it is the best warrant not to confuse the two.

The present chapter consists of three parts. First I elaborate some fundamental thoughts about sacredness while referring to two modalities of phenomenology. One is represented by Martin Heidegger (1889–1976) and can be rightly called philosophical; the other one is represented by Rudolf Otto (1869–1937) and Mircea Eliade (1907–86), whose work is subsumed under what one used to call the humanities (*Geisteswissen-schaften*) and, more particularly, to the (interdisciplinary) study of religion(s). However, both branches of phenomenology are centered around the question of the human being and can be characterized as fundamentally anthropological.[1] This double reference to phenomenology will enable me to lay bare a problematic aspect of a strictly anthropological approach to the sacred. Moreover, phenomenology sometimes inclines towards a reduction of phenomena which does not always (sufficiently) avoid the danger of ignoring history.

Therefore, the second section of the present chapter will be an excursion into the history of ideas. This excursion serves a double purpose. On the one hand, it shows that the theme of the sacred and its relation to salvation has known a certain development that drastically changed under the influence of modernity, though not in the way in which Heidegger and Eliade supposed it. On the other hand, this look into the history of ideas will allow me to profile in a much more nuanced way the task I will undertake in the third part: an examination of the profound connection between liturgy and salvation. The fundamental reason I elaborate on this question is that I am convinced that one will not arrive at an adequate understanding of the essence of the liturgy, neither by recuperating too hastily a vague revival of sensitivity for the sacred, nor by its opposite, that is,

---

1. For the very idea that there are different branches of phenomenology ensuing from the work of Edmund Husserl and that there is hence not a fundamental difference between Heidegger on the one side and Otto and Eliade on the other, I rely on the lucid philosophical analyses of Jean Greisch, *Le Buisson ardent et les Lumières de la raison: L'invention de la philosophie de la religion*, vol. II: *Les approaches phénoménologiques et analytiques* (Paris: Cerf, 2002). Regarding Eliade in particular, one additionally can refer to a specialized study: Douglas Allen, *Structure and Creativity in Religion: Hermeneutics in Mircea Eliade's Phenomenology and New Directions* (New York: Mouton Publishers, 1978), 107ff.

a too-rigid refutation or a massive rejection of the same sensitivity, as if it were irrelevant or harmful. The liturgy only shows what it really is through its deep insertion in the history and the economy of salvation. Therefore, the link between liturgy and soteriology deserves to be explored again, and deepened.

1. Sacredness and Humankind

Throughout the twentieth century, many thinkers have been interested in the phenomenon of the sacred. Some took it as the most fundamental category through which the true character of all religion can be grasped. Rudolf Otto, for example, in his famous 1917 study *Das Heilige* and with an obvious reference to Immanuel Kant, called the sacred the *a priori* category of religion.[2] The religious human being, *homo religiosus*, is the human being who is sensitive to sacredness, while the sacred is a dimension of being itself that both manifests and hides itself. It moreover affects human beings in the deepest layers of their existence. The effects of this affectedness can be both conscious or unconscious.

Heidegger: From Humanity to Divinity

In the philosophical sphere, Martin Heidegger is one of those thinkers who dealt with the sacred and saw in it a race to the divine, even if one is obliged to say that his attitude towards religion is very complex and ambiguous. In his renowned *Letter on Humanism*, he says:

> Only from the truth of being can the essence of the holy be thought. Only from the essence of the holy is the essence

---

2. Rudolf Otto, *The Idea of the Holy: An Inquiry into the Non-Rational Factor in the Idea of the Divine and its Relation to the Rational*, trans. John W. Harvey (Harmondsworth: Pelican Books, 1959).

of divinity to be thought. Only in the light of the essence
of divinity can it be thought or said what the word "God"
is to signify.[3]

This renowned quotation deserves to be meticulously discussed. I draw the attention to three aspects, which I not only explain but also criticize.

First, Heidegger designs a trajectory which takes being as the natural environment of the human *Dasein* as a point of departure, then passes through several consecutive levels and finally possibly culminates in "God." One wonders how Heidegger here avoids a contradiction with his own program of critical thinking and discernment, which aims at eliminating in metaphysics any remnant of onto-theology. For, according to this passage, it seems possible to move swiftly from being to God by the act of thinking.

Second, it is striking to observe that Heidegger's starting point is the investigation of the truth of being (*die Wahrheit des Seins*). Because this concept—not so much in its capacity as a concept alone—is of crucial importance for Heidegger (*a-lètheia*), one surmises that everything that follows is by no means evident. The one who poses the question of being itself (i.e., not the being of *a* being) is not sure that she will encounter the essence of the sacred (*das Wesen des Heiligen*). At the moment she encounters it, there will be no warrant that this discovery leads her to the true essence of the divine (*das Wesen*

---

3. Martin Heidegger, *Letter on 'Humanism,'* trans. Walter Kaufman, in *Pathmarks*, ed. William McNeill (Cambridge: Cambridge University Press, 1998), 239–76, 267. Here is the original text in German, which I am quoting because precise terminology matters: "Erst aus der Wahrheit des Seins läßt sich das Wesen des Heiligen denken. Erst aus dem Wesen des Heiligen ist das Wesen von Gottheit zu denken. Erst im Lichte des Wesens von Gottheit kann gedacht und gesagt werden, was das Wort, Gott' nennen soll." Martin Heidegger, *Brief über den Humanismus*, in *Wegmarken* (Frankfurt-am-Main: Vittorio Klostermann, 1996), 313–64, 351.

von Gottheit). And after all that, it still remains uncertain that in the light of this essence a trace of "God" can be indicated or observed. Hence, the continuity between being and God is highly unlikely, but to those who embark on a laborious journey and who stay open, receptive, and spontaneous in each and every step, God reveals Godself (maybe) in the horizon of being. Is it only for mystics, thinkers, and poets that God manifests himself?

Third, one must make mention of the context in which this quotation occurs, for it stems from a text devoted to a thorough reflection on the humanity of the human being. As one would expect, Heidegger firmly rejects any instance of a humanism that reduces the essence of the human being to something which must be justified on external grounds, for instance and most pointedly, to a being qualified along the lines of natural sciences and technocratic ideologies. For Heidegger, the human being is first of all the very specific place where the question of being opens itself in all its perplexity and complexity. It is most remarkable that Heidegger seems to have posed the question of God in the wake of the question of being. He even suggests that there is no other way:

> How can the human being at the present stage of world history ask at all seriously and rigorously whether the god nears or withdraws, when he has above all neglected to think into the dimension in which alone that question can be asked? But this is the dimension of the holy, which indeed remains closed as a dimension if the open region of being is not cleared and in its clearing is near to humans. Perhaps what is distinctive about this world-epoch consists in the closure of the dimension of the hale. Perhaps that is the sole malignancy.[4]

4. Heidegger, *Letter on 'Humanism,'* 267. Original version: "Wie soll denn der Mensch der gegenwärtigen Weltgeschichte auch nur ernst und streng fragen können, ob der Gott sich nahe oder entziehe, wenn der

Put differently, to attain God, one has no other option but to pass through the dimension of the sacred, but as a consequence of the historic and cultural circumstances in which modern human beings have found themselves, this access has been lost or covered over. Modern human beings calculate too much, control too much, master too much for them to still be affected by the immanent sacredness of being. Together with the poets, Heidegger tried to reopen, or keep open, this royal route to the sacred.

Eliade: Hierophanies

Even if his point of departure, his interest, and his method were not those of a philosopher of existence, Mircea Eliade, the famous historian of religion, formulates very similar ideas. Let us have a look at how he arrives at them.

For Eliade—as for Otto before him—there is no doubt that the human being qua human being is *homo religiosus*. This means that "the religious" is neither a free option nor an accidental quality. To the contrary, "the religious" is one of the factors constituting the ontological condition of the human being. Humanity has been religious in each culture and in each era. Human beings have always manifested religious behavior and have made religious gestures. It is only in modern Western civilization (especially in Europe, North America, and Australia) that a majority of the population seems to have become areligious.

Mensch es unterläßt, allererst in die Dimension hineinzudenken, in der jene Frage allein gefragt werden kann? Das aber ist die Dimension des Heiligen, die sogar schon als Dimension verschlossen bleibt, wenn nicht das Offene des Seins gelichtet und in seiner Lichtung dem Menschen nahe ist. Vielleicht besteht das Auszeichnende dieses Weltalters in der Verschlossenheit der Dimension des Heilen. Vielleicht ist dies das einzige Unheil" (Heidegger, *Brief über den Humanismus*, 351–52).

The content of the religious is circumscribed (or defined) by Eliade with the help of the concept of the sacred. It is through the manifestation of the sacred that human beings grasp something that infinitely transcends them.

> Man [*sic*] becomes aware of the sacred because it manifests itself, shows itself, as something wholly different from the profane. To designate the *act of manifestation* of the sacred, we have proposed the term *hierophany*. It is a fitting term, because it does not imply anything further; it expresses no more than is implicit in its etymological content, i.e., that *something sacred shows itself to us*. It could be said that the history of religions—from the most primitive to the most highly developed—is constituted by a great number of hierophanies, by manifestations of sacred realities.[5]

Eliade continues, but here we will have to make a detailed comment about the translation.

> From the most elementary hierophany—e.g., manifestation of the sacred in some ordinary object, a stone or a tree—to the supreme hierophany (which, for a Christian, is the incarnation of God in Jesus Christ) there is no solution of continuity.[6]

This strange collocation "solution of continuity" is a literal translation of the French *solution de continuité*, which means an interruption or a hiatus, the dissolving of a bond of continuity. Hence, when the French text says there is no such dissolving of the continuity, it actually means that there is *continuity*. The original version of the text, which was in German, confirms

5. Mircea Eliade, *The Sacred and the Profane: The Nature of Religion*, trans. Willard R. Task (New York: Harper & Row, 1961), 11.

6. Eliade, *The Sacred and the Profane*, 11.

this; it speaks of an "*ununterbrochene Kontinuität*,"[7] literally an uninterrupted continuity.

This idea of continuity is comparable to what Heidegger expressed through the track from being to God. In the framework of this trajectory or line of continuity, the sacred functions as an area of multiple mediations. The sacred shows itself at the intersection of immanence and transcendence, the down-here and the up-there, the natural and the supernatural. Eliade references a "dialectic of hierophanies."[8] In every manifestation of the sacred, a principle of elucidation that leads from obscurity to enlightenment is operative. Moreover, nothing is excluded from this dialectic; the sacred can manifest itself everywhere and through anything, through stones as well as through the most elevated writings and even through living persons. Eliade hastens to add, however, that this manifestation can by no means be boiled down to pantheism, so he forges the concept of "panontism," which I tend to interpret as asserting that there is nothing in being that cannot receive the status or the quality of the sacred. This panontism implies a strong realism: "Sacredness is, above all, *real*. The more religious a man is the more real he is, and the more he gets away from the unreality of a meaningless change. Hence man's tendency to 'consecrate' his whole life."[9]

Eliade asks himself the question how it has come and how one can explain that the modern human being has neglected this. He sees himself confronted with a paradox. On the one hand, modern human beings have not ceased to be human, and if the human being qua being human is religious (which is the presup-

7. Mircea Eliade, *Das Heilig und das Profane* (Hamburg: Rowohlt Taschenbuch Verlag, 1957), 8.

8. Mircea Eliade, *Patterns in Comparative Religion*, trans. Rosemary Sheed (New York: Sheed & Ward, 1958), 465. The original version of this monograph was entitled *Traité d'histoire des religions* (Paris: Payot, 1949).

9. Eliade, *Patterns in Comparative Religion*, 459.

position of the discourse on the *homo religiosus*), modern human beings cannot but be religious, too, in one way or another. On the other hand, it is impossible to deny the facts. Modern men and women have fundamentally distanced themselves from religion. What had always and everywhere been exceptional, a strange and asocial attitude or the reaction of an isolated individual (or of a small group only), has become in and through modernity the mentality of the masses. The existential areligious attitude has been vulgarized. In any case, modern women and men no longer respond to the criteria of the religious which Eliade himself formulated in the following way:

> Whatever the historical context in which he is placed, *homo religiosus* always believes that there is an absolute reality, *the sacred*, which transcends this world but manifests itself in this world, thereby sanctifying it and making it real. He further believes that life has a sacred origin and that human existence realizes all of its potentialities in proportion as it is religious—that is, participates in reality.[10]

Put differently, either one of the following possibilities is the case: either the irreligiosity of modern human beings inaugurates a new human species (which would be absurd) or their inevitable religiosity manifests itself more subtly.

Eliade solves this paradox through a conceptual enlargement (technically speaking, through a "formalization") of religious experience, but thereby inserts a structural ambiguity. The persistent resistance to the sacred hence becomes part of the immersion of humans in sacredness. This resistance

> appears even at the very heart of religious experience. Man's ambivalent attitude towards the sacred, which at

10. Eliade, *The Sacred and the Profane*, 202.

once attracts and repels him, is both beneficent and dangerous, can be explained not only by the ambivalent nature of the sacred in itself, but also by man's natural reactions to this transcendent reality which attracts and terrifies him with equal intensity.[11]

Consequently,

Nonreligious man in the pure state is a comparatively rare phenomenon, even in the most desacralized of modern societies. The majority of the "irreligious" still behave religiously, even though they are not aware of the fact. We refer not only to the modern man's many "superstitions" and "tabus," all of them magico-religious in structure. But the modern man who feels and claims that he is nonreligious still retains a large stock of camouflaged myths and degenerated rituals.[12]

This latter observation leads Eliade to a critical position vis-à-vis his contemporaries, which is again a maneuver similar to Heidegger's intellectual evolution. Modern women and men no longer demonstrate any respect for the mystery (of being) that surpasses them. Eliade provides an illustration:

It is not enough, as it was half a century ago, to discover and admire the art of Negroes and or Pacific islanders: we have now to rediscover the spiritual sources of these arts in ourselves; we must become aware of what it is, in a modern existence, that is still "mythical," and survives as such simply because this, too, is part and parcel of the

---

11. Eliade, *Patterns in Comparative Religion*, 460. In this quotation one clearly notices the massive influence Rudolf Otto exerted on Eliade's oeuvre. Eliade discussed the fact that he owes a great deal to his infamous predecessor in the field of the study of religions, e.g., at the very outset of *The Sacred and the Profane*, 8–10.

12. Eliade, *The Sacred and the Profane*, 204.

human condition, in that it expresses the anxiety of man living in Time.[13]

Questions Regarding the Continuity Hypothesis

Yet, at the end of this section, which consisted in a quick survey of what anthropology, in its double phenomenological figure, reveals about the notion of the sacred, it is only but appropriate to raise some questions. First, has the relationship between the human condition, being and the sacred been adequately conceived of? Second, is modernity indeed a desacralization of the world? Third, can one really approach the core of Christian liturgy through the theme of the sacred inherent in being? And finally, but this question could be the most surprising one (though for me it is the most penetrating one): what about salvation? Where should one situate it in all these analyses?

As to the first question, I think there are few reasons to cast doubt on the central conviction of phenomenology, namely that a certain sensitivity for the sacred is part of the human condition. It is likely that this sensitivity is truly a universal phenomenon, though it is and remains an assumption which is difficult to prove. There are many empirical data *pro*, and the empirical evidence *contra* is weak, limited and disputable. However, it is doubtful whether the category of the empirical and the appeal to data are at all helpful here. One could content oneself with the following observation: there aren't that many thinkers who obstinately deny the fact that people testify of unexplainable dimensions in being, and for that very reason one has to take seriously their testimonies.

13. Mircea Eliade, *Myths, Dreams and Mysteries: The Encounter between Contemporary Faiths and Archaic Realities*, trans. Philip Mairet (London: Harvill Press, 1960), 38.

As to the second question, I have more hesitations. I don't think that modernity produces an increasing desacralization of the *Lebenswelt*. I do think that manifestations of the sacred—hierophanies in the sense of Eliade—realize themselves according to modes that significantly differ from the ways this occurred prior to the development of modernity, but I would not equate this shift with desacralization. It is particularly disputable to look for and to discern different degrees or stages of sacredness. In any case, it is as advisable to be more prudent than phenomenology, and in addition to consider what the history of ideas can contribute in this respect.

The third question attempts to sound the relation between the sacred and the liturgy. Heidegger refused to give any religious content to his explanations of the sacred—which for some theological commentators has always been difficult to grasp, and which has moreover raised suspicions about Heideggerian meditations, although they are lucid and perspicuous.[14] In his turn, Eliade did not really consider liturgy, instead discussing at large the rites and cult of Christians. In them, he saw parallels with other religious traditions as well as reminiscences of ancient civilizations. This very approach has offered considerable insights for research and reflection, but a deeper approach to the liturgy would make use of this external perspective while also doing justice to the familiar, intimate nature of worship.[15]

The latter remark leads me to the fourth question, which lays bare a *Heilsvergessenheit* in the exploration of *Sein* and *das Heilige*. Both Heidegger and Eliade have forgotten about salvation, so that one does not know actually whether it shows itself *through* being or not. It surely shows itself *in* being, that is, within the milieu of beings, and *in* the existence of human

---

14. Emilio Brito, *Heidegger et l'hymne du sacré*, BETL 141 (Leuven: Leuven University Press, 1999).

15. Paul De Clerck , *L'intelligence de la liturgie* (Paris: Cerf, 2005).

persons, relations between them, and surroundings around them. But it may be possible that the origin of salvation is not being qua being itself in a way similar to being's situation at the origin of the discovery of the sacred. Perhaps one has to incorporate that origin beyond being as well if one wants to arrive at liturgy.

Let us now clarify these ideas, first with a reference to the history of ideas, after which we will turn to a proper theological perspective.

2. Modernity and Sacredness

According to the anthropologists, the idea of the sacred is of all times. However, rather paradoxically, the history of ideas does not seem to play a major role in their theories. Of course, they know that shapes of the sacred and the circumstances in which the sacred manifests itself have not always been identical. They realize that one has to put things into perspective and that discourses about an absolute infinity have definitely and definitively lost their power. They nonetheless lack a certain refinement when it comes to estimating and evaluating the influence of history. For history is not only that which determines the present context, the soil, as it were, of everything which happens today, or the necessary background of every process of appearing (that is to say, the condition of possibility for phenomenality: that there are phenomena). History itself has a history. History's ontological significance does not only consist in the fundamental recognition that there is a past (present) but also in that this past has passed through several formation phases and that history is always concrete and particular.

In the second section of this chapter I again rely on the investigations of Louis Dupré, professor emeritus at Yale University, and besides, a philosopher of great renown and an eminent expert of the history of ideas. His ideas will be instrumental for me to demonstrate that radical shifts pertaining to the attitude of human beings vis-à-vis being have occurred throughout the history of ideas. A nuanced comprehension of these shifts is indispensable for those who want to understand the essence of the liturgy in the contemporary world. Dupré's work doubtlessly yields penetrating insights into the intricacies of the sacred, salvation, the subject, modernity, and the particularity of Christianity.

Dupré is interested in the emergence of modernity because he envisages an encompassing understanding of the present cultural situation of the West, and thereby envisions the broadest possible notion of "culture." According to him, there is no study of the past, let alone of the history of ideas, without the desire and/or the intention to better understand the present. Moreover, in these endeavors religion plays a premier role—which, it must be said, is not equally the case for all his colleagues. In addition, Dupré does not share the massive scorn of modernity that unites many thinkers of postmodernity in spite of the insurmountable divergences among them. In their disdain, these thinkers distinguish themselves from a previous generation that did not camouflage its enthusiasm for modernity's accomplishments and even considered these achievements the definitive results of an unstoppable evolution.

> While they [the previous generation] exalted rational objectivity, moral tolerance, and individual choice as cultural absolutes, we now regard these principles with some suspicion. Undoubtedly there are good reasons to distrust the equation of the real with the objectifiable, progress with technological advances, and liberty of thought with detachment from tradition and social bonds. But should we attribute all such excesses to the original principles of modern culture?[16]

---

16. Louis Dupré, *Passage to Modernity: An Essay in the Hermeneutics of Nature and Culture* (New Haven: Yale University Press, 1993), 1.

Dupré's response to the latter question is a very firm and conscious "no." To the contrary, one has to know that modernity has never been and is not a monolithic movement. Enmity towards (institutional) religion and its attachment to the sacred are certainly not common features of modernity. This perspective would help many a theologian who deals with questions pertaining to modernity and postmodernity. On the one hand, it is an illusion to aspire the elimination of modernity. On the other hand, one has to acknowledge that there are many good modern things.

According to Dupré one has to distinguish (at least) three waves in the development of modern culture.[17] Each one of them bears consequences for the relation of human beings towards religion and the sacred.

The first wave emerged at the end of the fourteenth century under the mutual influence of the Renaissance (in Italy) and nominalist theology: "Only when the early humanist notion of human creativity came to form a combustive mixture with the negative conclusions of nominalist theology did it cause the cultural explosion that we refer to as modernity."[18] Hence, it is not the so-called natural sciences that are at the origin of the modern paradigm. The sciences themselves could only be born in a culture already marked by modernity. And, to be sure, it was not the sciences as such who would have destroyed the sensitivity for the sacred.

The second wave of modernity by and large covers the period between the Peace of Westphalia (1648) and the French Revolution (1789). It is the century of the Enlightenment. In his profound monograph on the Enlightenment, Dupré convincingly argues that this period also was not, in principle, against religion:

17. See chapter 2.
18. Dupré, *Passage to Modernity*, 3. Central aspects of Dupré's theory show striking similarities with the position of Hans Blumenberg as developed in his famous *Die Legitimität der Neuzeit*.

Even in its attitude towards religion, which has most se-
verely been criticized, the Enlightenment deserves considerable credit. Religious tolerance; the separation
between cult and public life; the protection of the individual conscience against religious compulsion, social
pressure, or cultural prejudice—all of these have become
nonnegotiable positions to Western believers. . . . The
critique of religion proved painful, particularly in the
irreverent form in which it was often administered; yet
it was necessary and overdue. In the end religion profited
from it. It forced the religious community to seek the
proper domain of religion in symbols of transcendence
rather than in science, and compelled it to begin a search
for the kind of spiritual depth needed to live in accordance with this insight.[19]

Finally, the third wave was given shape at the beginning of
the nineteenth century with the emergence of romanticism.[20]
Romanticism, too, was modern all-throughout and, as the two
previous waves, it continues to exert a considerable influence
on our cultures and societies.[21] Dupré adds that there is not a
necessary or logical link between these three phases. Hence it
would be erroneous to reduce them to one single principle, idea,
characteristic, or phenomenon only. It is only by keeping them
together that one has access to a full understanding of modernity. That which marks the modern human being most funda-

19. Louis Dupré, *The Enlightenment and the Intellectual Foundations of
Modern Culture* (New Haven: Yale University Press, 2004), 338–39.

20. Louis Dupré, *The Quest of the Absolute: Birth and Decline of European
Romanticism* (Notre Dame: University of Notre Dame Press, 2013). This
book finishes Dupré's trilogy on modernity.

21. See in this context the thought-provoking reflections of Dutch philosopher of culture Maarten Doorman, *De romantische orde* (Amsterdam:
Bakker, 2004), and a collective volume by Nikolas Kompridis, ed., *Philosophical Romanticism* (New York: Routledge, 2006).

mentally is, according to Dupré, a certain *isolation*, which is both fruitful and tragic. This isolation is caused by human beings themselves and cannot be easily suppressed or undone. The greatest difference between modern human beings and medieval and ancient human beings is that the latter two groups saw themselves embedded in a world in which humankind, nature, and God interpenetrated each other constantly and indissolubly. Diverse forms of modernity have contributed to disconnect human beings from this dynamic synthesis. The human being has slowly become the unique source of meaning, as Dupré has repeatedly expounded.[22] This is the most fundamental condition of all formidable achievements of modernity, but at the same time the modern human being is left alone. Humans have become the only speakers in being; it is in the end only their proper voices they hear. Being itself, nature, and God no longer speak to them—at least, that is what they believe and suppose they *must* believe. Evidently, this new ontological position entails burdensome consequences for the relation between the human being and the sacred and, therefore, also for the way in which Christianity is perceived. For this religion distinguishes itself by its message of a universal salvation that does not originate from the human imagination but comes from God.

Taking Dupré's thinking one step further, one could conclude that modernity does not equate to a radical *desacralization*, which implies that the sacred would disappear, but a profound *resacralization*, which means that the sacred appears differently. Modern human beings might recognize the sacred—and they are obviously still capable of venerating things—but they presuppose that it is the human mind which is at the origin of the sacred. For they have practically excluded

22. Dupré, *The Enlightenment*, 336; *Religion and the Rise of Modern Culture* (Notre Dame: Notre Dame University Press, 2008), 114–15; *Passage to Modernity*, 24.

all the other players in the domain of being. It is, moreover, this presupposition that makes impossible any authentic recognition or (re)discovery of salvation.

So what needs to be done? To save the sacred and the liturgy, should we (try to) become premodern again, as several philosophers and theologians have suggested? Is there not a problem with Dupré himself, inasmuch as he defends the legitimacy of modernity but at the same time contends that modernity has rejected the most fundamental characteristic of the sacred, that it comes from elsewhere?[23] And, consequently, must one not eliminate reason if one wants to preserve accesses to the sacred?

Dupré's answers to these questions are as nuanced as they are subtle. First, he says, the problem with modernity is not rationalism or universalism but the presumption that everything depends on the human mind. As a consequence, "a broader idea of reason is needed, one in which rationality is conceived as being in accordance with the order inherent in the nature of things."[24] A realistic metaphysics can indicate a path out of the modern crisis, but only inasmuch as it does not limit itself to the human mind to discover and determine truth. For

> the danger in restricting reason to the human mind is that it reduces reason to an instrument in the hands of human subjects. *Theoria* then comes to stand in the service of an all too easily self-directed *praxis*. The goals set by a program of rationalist universality seldom reflect the concrete order of reality, but rather reflect those set by *particular* events.[25]

23. Dupré asks himself similar questions, as e.g. in his book *Symbols of the Sacred* (Grand Rapids, MI: Eerdmans, 200), 121: "Is the modern mind still capable of creating effective religious symbols, or even of properly understanding those inherited from the past?"

24. Dupré, *Religion and the Rise*, 38.

25. Dupré, *Religion and the Rise*, 38.

For that matter, the Christian faith, its universal message as well as its practices advance an inherence in the concrete order of reality, for it is in that order that God himself has intervened by his incarnation. The multiple and variegated symbolic relations within this very act are founded and implied in being, in the most concrete reality, as all symbolic relations ultimately have to be ontological ties, if they are not to be unmasked as fantasies.

Christian liturgy participates in a reality which is at once immanent and transcendent. The immanent dimension guarantees that one does not have to do with something merely imagined, whereas the transcendent dimension guarantees the connection with the divine origin.

> The salvific influence of the sacramental action [a term which one could justifiably replace with "the liturgy"] does not originate in the nature of the rite considered in itself, as is the case in magic. Rather does the rite partake in a transcendent reality from which it derives an efficacy surpassing its ordinary power.[26]

To the extent that modernity still recognizes sacredness, in its most radical forms it rejects the two aforementioned dimensions: the ontological anchoring as well as the theological source of liturgy. Modernity tends to reduce liturgy to a performance directed by an inner-worldly volition and imagination.

So from the side of the modern human being nothing else but a radical conversion imposes itself, a conversion—let us repeat and emphasize it—that means modernity does not need to be abandoned altogether.

> The immediate question is . . . whether we are of a disposition to accept any kind of theoretical or practical direction coming from a source other than the mind itself.

---

26. Dupré, *Symbols of the Sacred*, 23.

> Such disposition demands that we be prepared to aban-
> don the conquering, self-sufficient state of mind charac-
> teristic of late modernity. . . . What is needed is a
> conversion to an attitude in which existing is more than
> taking, acting more than making, meaning more than
> function—an attitude in which there is enough leisure for
> wonder and enough detachment for transcendence.[27]

I think there are excellent reasons to call this conversion a truly
liturgical or sacramental conversion.

3. Liturgy and Soteriology

In the conclusion of *Symbols of the Sacred*, Louis Dupré expresses two particularly useful ideas for the problem at hand.
First, he maintains that reason is capable of conceiving the idea
of transcendence but that it is incapable of charging it with a
positive content.[28] Second, he holds that the need for religious
symbols is universal but that their nature and appearance are
always, necessarily, particular.[29] Accordingly, when I now
develop a reflection about the liturgy from a soteriological
angle, this is meant to be both an intelligent demonstration of
its transcendent dimension—which, we saw, is indispensable—and an indication of the particularity of the Christian
faith. I will structure my reflections around three lines of
thought. It is deliberate that I call them "lines of thought," for
they are not (yet) sufficiently elaborate. They are merely based
on some central theological intuitions. There is no doubt they
would require more specification and that they have to be
supported by more research and critique.

1. The first line of thought starts from a certain tension between revelation and salvation. However, one must note that

27. Dupré, *Religion and the Rise*, 117.
28. Dupré, *Symbols of the Sacred*, 124.
29. Dupré, *Symbols of the Sacred*, 127.

such a tension does not have its origin in theology itself. Rather, it is the consequence of the modern impulse to distinguish and separate all that is into discrete categories, in other words, of modernity's "logic of division."[30] Modern human beings generally still acknowledge there are things that surpass them and even that there are things which possibly reveal themselves to them. But at the same time they seem no longer willing to recognize that, at an existential level (and thus ontologically), they are destitute beings who are in need of salvation by a personal and transcendent God—a God by whom the human being is loved before they themselves can (start to) love and know Him. In other words, I think that one has approached modernity in too modern a manner. One has endeavored to objectify it, to grasp it to deal with it as comfortably as possible, to do justice to it as an accomplished fact, to embrace it always more intimately until one no longer feels its sharpest sides, to pack and wrap it in a box which can be easily transported or shipped wherever one goes.

One can rightly ask whether this attitude has been the best possible strategy but also whether it allowed for the deepest confrontation with modernity. I think that, at least from a theological point of view, the major problem with modernity is not primarily of an *epistemological* kind but of a *soteriological* nature.[31] To prove God's existence and to stipulate the conditions under which a knowledge of God can be meaningfully asserted are not the most profound problems. Instead, what is most profound is the very recognition of the need for grace and salvation.

Therefore, one should go one step further than Dupré. Of course one first needs a conversion—a point of encounter with real transcendence. But this move, however necessary and

---

30. What this logic of division is and how it is distinctive of a modern mindset is more elaborately explained in my essay, " 'Cogitor ergo sum': On the Meaning and Relevance of Baader's Theological Critique of Descartes," *Modern Theology* 21 (2005): 237–51.

31. See chapter 6.

desirable, must be complemented by an openness for that which comes from God. Without such an openness, this conversion risks developing itself only at a cognitive level. One has to open the heart for salvation. It does not suffice to acknowledge God exists and that He has addressed and is addressing human beings. One has to existentially comprehend and feel what He wanted to do and say: that He saves us because on our own we would never be capable of realizing the liberation from our own misery. We would never be able to efface our own sins.

This being said, I am convinced that the revival of the liturgy depends both on going beyond an overly epistemological focus of, and on, modernity and on an existential awareness that human beings need a God who has promised always to be there to assist them along the stages of their lives and to effectuate ultimate reconciliation with himself. A simple revival of the sense of sacredness, regardless of how authentic and intense it is, will always be too weak and too limited to undergird the liturgy until the eschaton. Without any doubt, such a revival can support the cause of Christian faith and liturgy but it cannot found and inspire them. The liturgy, moreover, is precisely there to save us from the spontaneous acknowledgment of the sacred, for, being *menschlich allzu menschlich*, we will always be too much involved in these acts of recognition. At some point we can always start to believe that everything depends on us. By directing our attention to Father, Son and Holy Spirit, the liturgy uplifts our capacity for veneration. The liturgy not only makes us recognize the Trinity but capacitates and facilitates genuine prayer for the praise and glory of the Lord and for the salvation of the world and all his holy church.[32]

2. The second line of thought is very closely intertwined with the previous one. It consists in viewing the liturgy in its

---

32. This phrase is an allusion to the euchological formula said at the conclusion of the Rite of the Preparation of the Gifts, e.g., right before the Prayer over the Gifts. See *The Roman Missal*.

actual active mode, or, as Louis-Marie Chauvet famously said, its "-*urgical*" nature. Liturgy is a lively continuation in word and deed both of God's revelation and/in the salvific work of Jesus Christ. One will not be surprised that I therefore add that the liturgy must be perseverant, courageous, and even a little stubborn.

In this context it is meaningful to refer to a famous line from Pope Leo the Great, which is quoted by great theologians who said important things about liturgy, such as Odo Casel, Edward Schillebeeckx, and Aidan Kavanagh, among others. Even the *Catechism of the Catholic Church* quotes the line: *Quod itaque Redemptoris nostri conspicuum fuit, in sacramenta transivit* ("what was to be seen in our Redeemer has passed over into the Sacraments").[33] One of the striking elements in this quotation is the major characteristic with which Leo the Great refers to Christ, namely as Redeemer. In so doing, he moreover seems to very accurately rephrase the first verses of the First Letter of John, where both the redeeming quality of the revelation and the revelatory dimension of salvation are expressed.

> We declare to you what was from the beginning, what we have heard, what we have seen with our eyes, what we have looked at and touched with our hands, concerning the word of life—this life was revealed, and we have seen it and testify to it, and declare to you the eternal life that was with the Father and was revealed to us—we declare to you what we have seen and heard so that you also may have fellowship with us; and truly our fellowship is with

33. The *Catechism* has "what was visible in our Savior has passed over into his mysteries" (1115). For a detailed commentary on this adage as well as its reception among chief representatives of the liturgical movement, see my contribution, "Paschal Joy Continued: Exploring Leo the Great's Theology of Christ's Ascension into Heaven," in *Preaching After Easter: Mid-Pentecost, Ascension, and Pentecost in Late Antiquity*, ed. Rich Bishop, Johan Leemans, and Hajnalka Tamas (Boston: Brill, 2016), 386–404.

the Father and with his Son Jesus Christ. We are writing
these things so that our joy may be complete. (1 John
1:1-4)

God's presence in the liturgy affects human beings in their
totality and effectuates there a joy that surpasses mere pleasure
by far. In order to realize that joy, the liturgy affects the senses
no less than human intelligence, their wills, their desires, their
bodies, their reason, and their very being-together or *Mitein-
andersein* (for in the liturgy God does not approach us as indi-
viduals first). In addition, God does not merely reveal himself
to us—something which could, theoretically, be interpreted in
fairly abstract terms—but graciously draws nearer and nearer,
very concretely, with a free offer of grace and salvation, and
does this through words and gestures, fragrances and colors,
sounds and images. Nevertheless, the liturgy does not receive
a sacred sense and meaning by virtue of the simple fact that it
employs cultic and cultural expressions of humans. Its sacramental sense and meaning are due to a foundational *anamnetic*
and *epicletic* aspect: the liturgy commemorates and thereby (re)
actualizes the salvific and redemptory actions of the Son of
God—not ours—and it invokes the Holy Spirit's pledge, so
that everything that it undertakes is marked by God's—not
our—seal.

3. The third line of thought evokes and reflects on the "meta-
sacred" nature that characterizes the liturgy. For one cannot
deny that the liturgy, precisely because it entails Christ's actions, is marked by an eminent kind of sacredness. Already in
the introduction of the present chapter I said that I by no means
favor a separation between notions of sacred and salvation.
Here I add that the sacredness of the liturgy is "meta-sacred"
because it is a sacredness "from above" rather than one "from
below." It is not a sacredness rooted in the spontaneous propensity of humans to be trembled, troubled, stupefied but also
fascinated and intrigued by something in nature that tran-

scends them. It is a highly cultured sacredness, actually more a sacramentality, which presupposes a profound familiarity with the customs, the content, and the many meanings of the liturgy—and, thus, a personal relationship with God. Rowan Williams captures this very well when he straightforwardly contends:

> Sacramentality is not a general principle that the world is full of "sacredness"; it is the very specific conviction that the world is full of the life of a God whose nature is known in Christ and the Spirit. The meaning we make in all our creative activity has to be informed by this kind of holiness.[34]

For all these reasons it may be more appropriate to talk about the holiness rather than the sacredness of the liturgy. The famous distinction between the adjectives *sacred* (in French, *sacré*) and *holy* (in French, *saint*)[35] serves to evoke the necessary connection that exists between liturgy and faith on the one hand, and God on the other. Christians (are invited to) believe and pray (*lex orandi, lex credendi*) that God's holiness is ultimately the source of the transformation of the world's sacredness. As the German scholar of French and comparative literature Peter-Eckhard Knabe lucidly explains,

34. Rowan Williams, Foreword in *The Gestures of God: Explorations in Sacramentality*, ed. Geoffrey Rowell and Christine Hall (New York: Continuum, 2004), xiii.

35. Emmanuel Levinas wrote a fascinating book entitled *Du sacré au saint: Cinq nouvelles lectures talmudiques* (Paris: Minuit, 1977). He additionally used the same distinction between sacredness and sainthood to criticize Heidegger. See also Jean Greisch, *Le Buisson ardent et les Lumières de la raison. L'invention de la philosophie de la religion,* Tome III: *Vers un paradigme herméneutique* (Paris: Cerf, 2004), 717–20. Apparently, Jean Greisch defends Heidegger, whereas I would side with Levinas—and Jean-Yves Lacoste, for that matter—on this point.

> the sacred [*le sacré*] supposes . . . a particular, venerable and untouchable quality, for which it is right to fight. The object of worship is by no means God here, but a kind of substitute for him which separates the world in two parts: a quotidian one—the one of the profane—and another one, to which the sacred gives its intimate meaning.[36]

Clearly, it is not in this respect that the liturgy would be sacred.

> As a matter of fact, the holy [*saint*] concerns objects and persons which are chosen by divine grace and which possess a distinctive trait which, inasmuch as it removes one from other human beings, simultaneously draws them nearer to God. Similar things can be said about poets and priests as well as about those places where they lived. Because God himself is beyond his creatures, it is to him that the term holy [*saint*] applies. The use of the latter, therefore, can by no means be conceived without reference to God.[37]

Thus, the liturgy is much rather holy than sacred and it shares this sainthood with the Church. Holiness unites and reconciles, whereas sacredness marks differences and separates.

36. Peter-Eckhard Knabe, "Signifaction de sacré," in *Le sacré: Aspects et manifestations. Études publiées in memoriam Horst Baader*, ed. Peter-Eckhard Knabe , Jürgen Rolshoven, and Margarethe Stracke (Tübingen—Paris: Günther Narr—Jean-Michel Place, 1982), 11–22, here at 12 (my translation, JG).

37. Knabe, "Signification de sacré," 12 (my translation, JG).

PART II

Positioning the World in the Liturgy

The liturgy, through which "the work of our redemption takes place," especially in the divine sacrifice of the Eucharist, is supremely effective in enabling the faithful to express in their lives and portray to others the mystery of Christ and the real nature of the true church. For the church is both human and divine, visible but endowed with invisible realities, zealous in action and dedicated to contemplation, present in the world, yet a migrant, so constituted that in it the human is directed toward and subordinated to the divine, the visible to the invisible, action to contemplation, and this present world to that city yet to come, the object of our quest . . . The liturgy daily builds up those who are in the church, making of them a holy temple of the Lord, a dwelling-place for God in the Spirit . . . , to the mature measure of the fullness of Christ . . . At the same time it marvellously enhances their power to preach Christ and thus show the church to those who are outside as a sign lifted up among the nations . . . , a sign under which the scattered children of God may be gathered together . . . until there is one fold and one shepherd.

—*Sacrosanctum Concilium* 2

CHAPTER 4

Liturgy, Desacralization and Sanctification

There seems to be a growing consensus that the strained relationship between faith and culture is not solely a problem of language, as many liturgists and theologians have nonetheless assumed for quite some time.[1] Today there is a keen awareness that the vernacular languages in which liturgies have been celebrated since the liturgical reforms issuing from the Second Vatican Council will never coincide with ordinary speech. One additionally realizes that the accessibility of liturgy and sacraments does not—or at least does not *exclusively*—depend on a willingness or unwillingness to adapt, modify, or accommodate, to interpret the rites and texts of liturgical services, or on the question of whether or not these changes are sanctioned by competent authorities and implemented with pastoral success. In other words, there seems to be something strange going on in the liturgy.

The goal of this chapter is to shed light on that "strangeness" of the liturgy and to do that from a deliberately theological perspective. The guiding question is whether and, if so, to what degree, secularism has impacted on the self-understanding of liturgy and sacraments. This question may sound odd, since it is generally taken for granted that secularization processes have exerted a massive influence on the

---

1. Instructive in this respect is Paul De Clerck's analysis in the first chapter of his book, *L'intelligence de la liturgie* (Paris: Cerf, 2005).

77

church's ritual repertoire as well as on the experiences of the faithful. Nevertheless, there may be reasons to further inquire what exactly secularism has done to the celebration of the sacraments in modern and postmodern settings and what it has been unable to affect.

The underlying hypothesis of the following reflections is that it is much too simple to attribute phenomena like waning church attendance and liturgical richness to the process of secularization, as if that secularization had endangered, or even destroyed, the sacred character of Christian celebrations and ceremonies, and consequently, as a powerful token of one's being religious, one must stand firm against secularization's ongoing *desacralization* of the entire life-world of people. The truth is that liturgy itself can be understood as a powerful desacralizing reality. The difference with secularism may hence not be liturgy's distance towards or difference from natural sacredness but its goal and its vision. What liturgy ultimately tries to achieve, because it already participates in that dynamic, is the *sanctification* of the world, whether secular or not, postmodern or primitive, religious or atheistic. In a certain sense, liturgy maintains (and ought to maintain) a certain "in-difference" towards any characteristic of the world.

To build up the case appropriately, this chapter is divided into two parts, the first of which lays the basis for what is elaborated in greater detail in the second one. One could call the first part the negative one, in which the connection between liturgy and desacralization is investigated. The point of departure is Alexander Schmemann's bold claim that secularism is the "negation" of Christian worship.[2] This claim is critically evaluated and compared with a profound insight of Yves Congar. Correspondingly, the second part discusses in a positive way what

2. Alexander Schmemann, *For the Life of the World: Sacraments and Orthodoxy* (Crestwood, NY: St Vladimir's Seminary Press, 1973), 118, 124.

the connection is between liturgy and sanctification. I will again appeal to Schmemann to better understand how he sees the mutual relation between the church and the Eucharist from a liturgical and an eschatological point of view. These considerations will be supplemented by some more recent theological and philosophical scholarship that discusses the messianic dimension of the kingdom to come and its critical distance towards the world in which we live. On the basis of all that material I will draw some preliminary conclusions about the nature of the liturgy and make suggestions about the reasons liturgy and secularism may indeed be incommensurable, despite many well-intended attempts to bridge the gap.

1. Liturgy and Desacralization

Schmemann's Challenge

Schmemann observes that the phenomenon of secularism has caused deep division among Christians. Whereas some approach it entirely positively and welcome it as a blessing, others are far more reluctant and even take a somewhat inimical stance. "There are those who reduce the Church to the world and its problems, and those who simply equate the world with evil and morbidly rejoice in their apocalyptic gloom."[3] Clearly, Schmemann does not want to side with either alternative. He criticizes the first option, which treats the world as a reality independent from faith and liturgy. The second option is rejected because it actually turns its back to the world and does not seem to understand the implications of a theology of creation. In a certain sense, the opposite alternatives make the same mistake, in that they misconstrue the *relation* between liturgy and world, albeit with completely different consequences.

---

3. Schmemann, *For the Life of the World*, 8.

Precisely the notions of "creation" and "world," however, are of paramount importance to understand Schmemann's liturgical position. The liturgy takes place in the world as it was created by God. As such, it was never meant as a rejection of the world, even if, through original sin, there is something deeply wrong with the world and its inhabitants. According to Schmemann, liturgy insinuates itself into the world to make the world into a more beautiful tapestry;[4] it is not and ought never be considered a safe harbor that protects against the evils of the world. To think that such harmless harbors exist would be a gigantic illusion and eventually lead to mere disillusion. Even more, such suppositions may probably be called sinful, as they refuse to see the world as God's gift and creation.

But why is it, then, that Schmemann seems so harsh on secularism? The reason is that he sees secularism not as a system of thought that genuinely represents the interests of the world (there would be nothing wrong with that) but as an *ideology* that treats the world independent of God, faith, and religion. The problem is not that secularism tries to defend the world but that it does so by distancing itself from its own roots. Schmemann proposes the following working definition of secularism: it is "the progressive and rapid alienation of our culture, of its very foundations, from the Christian experience and 'world view' which initially shaped that culture."[5] Elsewhere he further explains: "Secularism—we must again and again stress this—is a 'stepchild' of Christianity, as are, in the last analysis, all secular ideologies which today dominate the world."[6]

---

4. The image of a tapestry is meaningfully elaborated in Hans Boersma, *Heavenly Participation: The Weaving of a Sacramental Tapestry* (Grand Rapids, MI: Eerdmans, 2011). Interestingly, Boersma refers to Schmemann (8–9) but his major source of inspiration is the *nouvelle théologie* and, in particular, the theology of Henri de Lubac. See chapter 5.

5. Schmemann, *For the Life of the World*, 7.

6. Schmemann, *For the Life of the World*, 127.

Even though this definition of secularism is quite ordinary and definitely determined by a context that reacted towards the ongoing processes of secularization in an apologetic way, that is, above all in terms of a "loss" (of sense and influence), it is important to stress the preeminently theological nature of Schmemann's dealings with secularism. Interestingly, he does interpret secularism as a "heresy," but not one about God or Christ—he realizes that "secularism is by no means identical with atheism"[7]—but is rather concerned with the human being. "It is the negation of man [*sic*] as a worshiping being, as *homo adorans*: the one for whom worship is the essential act which both 'posits' his humanity and fulfills it."[8] The category of *homo adorans* was introduced by Schmemann to indicate that the most fundamental calling of the human being was praying to and/ as sojourning in the intimate presence of God. But, again, that intimacy was interrupted by the first couple's disobedience and misplaced striving for independence.

Schmemann correspondingly understands the liturgy as the sacramental way in which, through the paschal mystery of the Redeemer, women and men are enabled (again) to repose in God's company. In other words, the liturgy for him is profoundly doxological and eschatological. But that is precisely the fundamental reason it maintains strained relationships with a secular understanding of time and space. Secularism cuts itself off from the deep connection between God and the human condition—a connection that was disturbed but never undone and, moreover, one for which God alone—not the human being—took the initiative to restore. Hence, it comes as no surprise that, according to Schmemann, "the real cause of *secularism*" is "ultimately nothing else but the affirmation of the world's autonomy, of its self-sufficiency in terms of

7. Schmemann, *For the Life of the World*, 124.
8. Schmemann, *For the Life of the World*, 118.

reason, knowledge, and action."[9] Secularism is both unable and unwilling to acknowledge the world's and humankind's *relation* with God and may therefore indeed be regarded as a blunt "negation" of worship.

Schmemann's bold statement raises the question of whether the apparent opposition between liturgy and secularism can be overcome, and more particularly, of their seemingly antagonistic approaches to the world. Is there continuity or discontinuity between the liturgy and the natural sense of sacredness with which human beings, even those living in secular cultures, would be naturally equipped? Somewhat surprisingly, Schmemann himself leaves open that question, inasmuch as he says that

> the uniqueness, the *newness* of Christian worship is not that it has no *continuity* with worship in "general," as some overly zealous apologists tried to prove . . . but that in Christ this very continuity is fulfilled, receives its ultimate and truly new significance so as to truly bring all "natural" worship to an end.[10]

At this point it is helpful to complement Schmemann's view with an intriguing insight of Congar.

Congar's Insight

In a volume which appeared in 1967 in the immediate aftermath of the promulgation of *Sacrosanctum Concilium* and which was edited by himself and his fellow Dominican brother Jean-Pierre Jossua, Yves Congar tackled the question of *where*

---

9. Schmemann, *For the Life of the World*, 129.
10. Schmemann, *For the Life of the Word*, 122.

the sacred fits into a Christian worldview.[11] At the outset of his text, Congar expresses a moderate sympathy for Eliade's work in the history of religions and the anthropology of religion, especially for *The Sacred and the Profane*,[12] but he significantly adds that Christianity is about "something completely different."[13] He thereupon engages in an interpretation of Old Testament and New Testament passages where it becomes clear that God's revelation and salvific plan are not concerned with maintaining a sacred order which is sharply distinguished from a profane one. To the contrary, the categories of the sacred and the profane as well as the very difference between them are of no use when it comes to understanding and explaining what Christian faith and sacraments effectuate and mean. It strikes Congar that the profane in particular seems to have no place in the logic of the Scriptures: "The Gospel abolishes the sacred as a kind of withdrawal from the world only by abolishing the category of the profane."[14] Hence, it "teaches us clearly enough that nothing is profane for the Christian, because everything can be sanctified. Everything that God has made is good."[15] In a manner not unlike Schmemann, Congar develops, or at least relies on, a theology of creation to make sense of Christian worship and liturgy.

11. Yves Congar, "Where Does the 'Sacred' Fit into a Christian Worldview?," in *At the Heart of Christian Worship: Liturgical Essays of Yves Congar*, trans. and ed. Paul Philibert (Collegeville, MN: Liturgical Press, 2010), 108–32. The French title of the essay is "Situation du 'sacré' en régime chrétien" and the original volume in which it appeared was volume 66 in the renowned Unam Sanctam series; it was published with Cerf in Paris.

12. Mircea Eliade, *The Sacred and the Profane: The Nature of Religion*, trans. Willard R. Trask (Orlando, FL: Harcourt, 1987). For a discussion of this work, see chapter 3.

13. Congar, "Where Does the Sacred," 108.

14. Congar, "Where Does the Sacred," 117.

15. Congar, "Where Does the Sacred," 121.

Thus, it seems that there is no natural or spontaneous continuity between the realm of world and history on the one hand and sacramental reality on the other, because creation and redemption do not coincide. "The world of grace, the source of our communion with God, is a distinct, original domain, never completely homogeneous with the world itself."[16] In this respect, moreover, Congar sides with the profound theological intuitions of his contemporaries Marie-Dominique Chenu and Louis Bouyer, who had argued that the human being is not in and of itself *liturgiefähig*.[17] As a human being, a woman or a man is not Christian but can only become one through entering into the liturgico-sacramental order of the Risen One, that is, through baptism.

Christian liturgy and sacraments share ontologically both in God's good creation and in Christ's redemptive work. Their reconnecting work is called sanctification but in no way coalesces with any "natural" sacredness. The reason is that in and through Christ's life, death, resurrection, and ascension the old cultic dividing lines have ceased to exist. They are no longer valid and have moreover been replaced by a much more powerful alternative, the Body of Christ. Congar is very firm on this: "There is only *one* sacred reality, the body of Christ"[18]— whereby he is aware that the use of the word "sacred" in this context is only analogous to the commonly known "sacreds." He explains: "Jesus Christ, to whom we become mystically incorporated and identified, is himself the fullness of sanctity, the Holy One of God. Every aspect of the question of the sacred needs to be seen in relation to Christ."[19]

---

16. Congar, "Where Does the Sacred," 125.

17. Marie-Dominique Chenu, "Anthropologie et liturgie," in *La Maison-Dieu* 12 (1947): 53–65; Louis Bouyer, *Le rite et l'homme. Sacralité naturelle et liturgie*, Lex orandi 32 (Paris: Cerf, 1962). Congar refers to both works in "Where Does the Sacred," 124.

18. Congar, "Where Does the Sacred," 126; see also 123.

19. Congar, "Where Does the Sacred," 128.

In sum, with a reference to both Schmemann and Congar, it seems fair to conclude that the liturgy has an unmistakable *desacralizing* dimension. Not only does it fail to coincide with natural sacredness, it puts it under critique. It does not do so, however, in a defying, repudiating, or derogatory mode, but with a clear invitation to join in the soteriological dynamic of the Christ event. In other words, it *sanctifies*.

2. Liturgy and Sanctification

Church and Eucharist

When the presider of the liturgical assembly uses the second eucharistic prayer of *The Roman Missal*, which is arguably the most frequently used in contemporary Catholicism, one hears God acclaimed as the *fons omnis sanctitatis* ("the fount of all holiness").[20] This happens immediately following the preface, so that the phrase somehow recaptures the solemn doxology of the Sanctus, the "Holy, Holy, Holy," What this powerful liturgical action implies at a theological level, is that there is no doubt whatsoever about the origin of sacredness, or sanctity. It is not the upheaval of something immanent in nature but the infusion of something transcendent or supernatural which, furthermore, does not destroy or render superfluous that which it permeates (see also the well-known Thomistic dictum *gratia non tollit naturam sed perficit*). As such, the liturgy respects and reinforces the fundamental provocative logic of Christian revelation.[21]

---

20. *The Roman Missal: English Translation According to the Third Typical Edition for Use in the Dioceses of the United States of America* (Collegeville, MN: Liturgical Press, 2011), 646 (no. 100).

21. For an account of the provocative nature of Christian revelation, see my *Revelation, Reason and Reality: Theological Encounters with Jaspers, Schelling and Baader*, Studies in Philosophical Theology 39 (Leuven: Peeters, 2007).

This infusion of meaning is realized most efficiently through the celebration of the Eucharist, which has no other purpose and mission than to connect, or reconnect again more solidly, the entire universe with its creator. The Eucharist is there to offer the real Body of Christ to humanity (sacramentally) so that humanity can reestablish itself as the true Body of Christ (ecclesially).[22] This intricate relationship has been paradigmatically explored by Alexander Schmemann.

For Schmemann, everything about the Eucharist is genuinely *sacramental*. In his famous study on the Eucharist, published posthumously, he discusses the entire course of its *ordo*—from the act of gathering and the entrance hymn until Communion and concluding prayers. Schmemann considers the Eucharist to be most fundamentally "the sacrament of the Kingdom,"[23] and extrapolates this to the liturgy as such: "The whole liturgy is to be seen as the sacrament of the Kingdom of God, the Church is to be seen as the presence and communication of the Kingdom that is to come."[24]

When dealing with the central part of the eucharistic celebration, the anaphora or eucharistic prayer, he lucidly underpins his emphatic choice to call everything a "sacrament" as follows:

> I see the entire task at hand in demonstrating as fully as possible that the divine liturgy is a single, though also "multifaceted," sacred rite, a single sacrament, in which

22. Henri de Lubac, *Corpus mysticum: The Eucharist and the Church in the Middle Ages: Historical Survey*, trans. Gemma Simmonds, et al. (London: SCM Press, 2006).

23. Alexander Schmemann, *The Eucharist: Sacrament of the Kingdom*, trans. Paul Kachur (Crestwood, NY: St Vladimir's Seminary Press, 1987).

24. Alexander Schmemann, "Liturgy and Eschatology," in *Liturgy and Tradition: Theological Reflections of Alexander Schmemann*, ed. Thomas Fisch (Crestwood, NY: St Vladimir's Seminary Press, 1990), 89–100, 95.

all its "parts," their entire sequence and structure, their coordination with each other, the necessity of each for all and all for each, manifests to us the inexhaustible, eternal, universal and truly divine meaning of what has been and what is being accomplished.[25]

It follows from this that the church's deepest vocation is to continue to realize, establish, and live up to its sacramentality, which she first receives from Christ before she can offer it to the world. The church's sacramental nature is a profoundly mysterious reality that precedes her but in which she at the same time ontologically shares, however, just like manna and sacramental grace, not in order to store it but to pass it on, present it, and "radiate" it always and everywhere.[26] Inasmuch as the church celebrates the Eucharist, the faithful

are made participants of the Messianic Banquet, of the New Pascha; it is from there, "having seen the true light, having received the heavenly Spirit," that [they] return into "this world" . . . as witnesses of the Kingdom which is "to come." Such is the sacrament of the Church, the *leitourgia* which eternally transforms the Church into what she is, makes her the Body of Christ and the Temple of the Holy Spirit.[27]

In other words, the church, inasmuch as she *actually* celebrates the Eucharist, is a powerful motor for the *transformation* of the world.

---

25. Schmemann, *The Eucharist*, 160–61.

26. See in this context the profound reflections of Louis-Marie Chauvet, *Symbol and Sacrament: A Sacramental Reinterpretation of Christian Existence*, trans. Patrick Madigan and Madeleine Beaumont (Collegeville, MN: Liturgical Press, 1995), 44–45.

27. Alexander Schmemann, "Theology and Eucharist," in *Liturgy and Tradition*, 69–88, 83.

> For the Eucharist . . . is a *passage*, a procession of the
> Church into "heaven," into her fulfillment as the King-
> dom of God. And it is precisely the reality of this passage
> into the *Eschaton* that conditions the transformation of
> our offering—bread and wine—into the new food of the
> new creation, of our meal into the Messianic Banquet and
> the *Koinonia* of the Holy Spirit.[28]

Apparently, for Schmemann, the entire celebration of the Eucharist can be considered consecratory. The consecration is not
limited to one individual rite but can (and should) be extended
to the sacrament as a whole. The fact that the church fathers
used the word *eucharistia* to indicate "both the prayer of consecration and the consecrated gifts"[29] is seen as a corroboration
of this idea.

Schmemann strongly criticizes those theological tendencies
which have led to a reduction of this broad understanding
of the transformational and consecratory dimension of the
Eucharist, which he thinks is especially manifest in Western
scholastic interpretations of transubstantiation. In his own
Orthodox tradition, he argues,

> the *metabole* itself—the change of the bread and wine into
> the Body and Blood of Christ—and the communion of
> the Holy Gifts are viewed as the fulfillment, the crowning
> point and the climax, of the whole Eucharistic liturgy,
> whose meaning is precisely that it *actualizes* the Church
> as the new creation, redeemed by Christ, reconciled with
> God, given access to heaven, filled with divine Glory,
> sanctified by the Holy Spirit, and *therefore* capable of and
> called to participation in divine Life, in the communion
> of the Body and Blood of Christ.[30]

---

28. Schmemann, "Theology and Eucharist," 82.
29. Schmemann, "Theology and Eucharist," 83.
30. Alexander Schmemann, *Of Water and the Spirit: A Liturgical Study
of Baptism* (Crestwood, NY: St. Vladimir's Seminary Press, 1974), 117.

Another word for "consecration" could be "sanctification." Through the Eucharist the Church connects herself and the world with the sanctifying dynamic that finds its origin in God's initiative of salvation. Therefore, it is important that the Church continuously acknowledges that the deepest roots of her ritual are not immanent but transcendent.

> The Church is not a natural community which is "sanctified" through the cult. In its essence the Church is the presence, the actualization in this world of the "world to come," in this *aeon*—of the Kingdom. And the mode of this presence, of this actualization of the new life, the new *aeon*, is precisely the *leitourgia*.[31]

The consequence of this position is as lucid as it is harsh: the liturgy entails "the abolishment of cult as such, or at least . . . the complete destruction of the old philosophy of cult."[32] The reason is that the cultic household, or ritual "economy," presupposed a radical distinction between sacred and profane, and that the maintenance of this distinction runs contrary to the unifying and reconciling dynamic intrinsic to the grand operation of grace, salvation, love, and sanctification in the Christian regime.[33]

Through this brief exploration of the intrinsic connection between church and Eucharist it has moreover become apparent that the concept of "time" is of eminent importance. Concretely, eschatology seems to be necessarily involved when one thinks through what sanctification in general and the sanctifying nature of liturgy and sacraments really are. Therefore, it is only but appropriate that we now shift the attention to the eschatological dimension of liturgy while bearing in mind the question how the liturgy relates to secular culture(s).

31. Alexander Schmemann, "Theology and Liturgical Tradition," in *Liturgy and Tradition*, 11–20, 16–17.
32. Schmemann, "Theology and Liturgical Tradition," 16.
33. See chapter 3.

The Messianic Kingdom

For Schmemann, it is evident that eschatology is by no means a flight from the world. Rather, eschatology sheds a light on the specific way of Christian inherence in, and habitation of the world: as the Gospel of John teaches in several instances, Christians are in the world, but not "of" the world.[34] Hence, it does not come as a surprise that Schmemann sees eschatology as a fundamental and all-pervasive dimension of Christian faith and theology; it is much more than a chapter in the book of faith which explains how Christians imagine "the last things."

> Eschatology has been transposed into personal hope, personal waiting. But in reality the whole of Christian theology is eschatological, and the entire experience of life likewise. It is the very essence of the Christian faith that we live in a kind of rhythm—leaving, abandoning, denying the word, and yet at the same time always returning to it; living in time by that which is beyond time; living by that which has not yet come, but which we already know and possess.[35]

According to Schmemann, it was above all a deeply eschatological awareness that shaped the identity of Christian faith and its ritual expression in liturgy and sacraments. He is not afraid to speak about a radical "change" in people's religiosity brought about by Christianity.[36] The very meaning of that

---

34. See in this context again the interesting reflections of Paul Valadier, *La condition chrétienne: du monde sans en être* (Paris: Seuil, 2003).

35. Schmemann, "Liturgy and Eschatology," 95.

36. Schmemann does not stand alone with this interpretation; it can be found among other liturgical theologians. See, e.g., Geoffrey Wainwright, *Doxology: The Praise of God in Worship, Doctrine, and Life: A Systematic Theology* (New York: Oxford University Press, 1984), 154: "There are hints

change, he argues, consisted "in the appearance of a new understanding of the cult, of a new liturgical piety wholly determined by the faith of Christians in the ontological newness of the Church as the eschatological beginning in this world, in this aeon, of the Aeon of the Kingdom."[37]

Schmemann specifies that this eschatological newness of the cultic life of Christians is not a "mediation between the sacred and the profane, but the fact of the accomplished consecration of the people by the Holy Spirit [and] their transformation into 'sons of God.' "[38] This powerful event of transformation is predominantly realized through the celebration of the Eucharist:

> By participating in His Supper Christians receive into themselves His life and His Kingdom, i.e., the New Life and the New Aeon. In other words, the eschatology of the Eucharist is not world renouncing, not a turning away from time, but above all the affirmation of the reality, the certainty and the presence of the Kingdom of Christ which is "within," which is already here within the Church, but which will be manifest in all glory only at the end of "this world."[39]

Schmemann underscores the "strangeness" of this Christian newness vis-à-vis pagan forms of rituality, which upheld forms

---

that the early Christians saw their eucharist as the successor of the Jewish passover, and this will account in part for the eschatologically charged atmosphere which surrounded the Christian sacrament from the first and which has never entirely disappeared." Historical observations and theological interpretations are interwoven here in quite emphatic a way.

37. Alexander Schmemann, *Introduction to Liturgical Theology*, trans. Asheleigh E. Moorehouse (Crestwood, NY: St Vladimir's Seminary Press, 2003), 102.

38. Schmemann, *Introduction to Liturgical Theology*, 103.

39. Schmemann, *Introduction to Liturgical Theology*, 73.

of piety based on a sharp difference between the sacred and the profane. The conservation and protection of this difference went along with "the understanding of the cult as primarily a system of ceremonies and ritual which transmits sacredness to the profane and establishes between the two the possibility of communion and communication." Schmemann correspondingly claims to

> know that Christianity set itself in opposition to the mystery religions on this point.[40] It professed salvation not as the possibility of an individual or even collective deliverance from evil and sin, it professed sanctification not as the possibility for the "profane" to touch the "sacred," but proclaimed both as the eschatological fulfillment of the history of salvation, as the event leading man [*sic*] into the Aeon of the Kingdom of God.[41]

As a consequence, the Eucharist is not so much to be understood as a mimetic operation which displays the incarnation or mimics the Last Supper Jesus held with his disciples. Rather it should be seen as "the manifestation of the Church as the new aeon" or "the lifting up of the Church into His *parousia*, the Church's participation in His heavenly glory."[42]

Yet, very interestingly, Schmemann's profoundly theological intuitions have found support from an unexpected angle. The Italian philosopher and political theorist Giorgio Agamben, who, as already mentioned, considers himself an atheist, re-

---

40. This reference to the ancient Greek mystery religions is obviously meant as a critical comment on the work of Odo Casel. For a recent theological discussion of Casel's work, see my contribution, "Meandering in Mystery: Why Theology Today Would Benefit from Rediscovering the Work of Dom Odo Casel," in *Mediating Mysteries, Understanding Liturgies: On Bridging the Gap Between Liturgy and Systematic Theology*, ed. Joris Geldhof (Leuven: Peeters, 2015), 11–32.

41. Schmemann, *Introduction to Liturgical Theology*, 126.

42. Schmemann, *Introduction to Liturgical Theology*, 72.

cently devoted a great amount of attention to the history of ideas and thereby uncovered many that can be traced back to a Christian origin.[43] Agamben demonstrates that modern democratic systems, including the bureaucracies undergirding them as well as the prevailing economical paradigm which increasingly permeates different spheres of life, are somehow rooted in Christian faith and worship. While he admits that "the thesis according to which the real Christian politics is liturgy and the Trinitarian doctrine founds politics as participation in the glorious worship of the angels and saints may appear surprising,"[44] he assembles a substantial quantity of material to support this line of argument and interprets the data convincingly.

Agamben's ideas at least raise the question what the relation is between liturgy and politics in a secular realm, especially in view of the etymology of the word *leitourgia* (public service). Inasmuch as he observes that "Christ coincides without remainder with his liturgy" and that "precisely this coincidence confers on his liturgy its incomparable efficacy,"[45] he is theologically well-informed, to say the least. The question of efficacy and the way it is managed and controlled is what fascinates him the most, as it functions as the essential link with present-day neoliberal economies.

> What defines the Christian liturgy is precisely the aporetic but always reiterated attempt to identify and articulate

43. The whole construction of Agamben's *Homo sacer* project must be left out of our scope here. For a thorough introduction to and discussion of his work from a theological perspective, see Colby Dickinson, *Agamben and Theology* (New York: T. & T. Clark, 2011).

44. Giorgio Agamben, *The Kingdom and the Glory: For a Theological Genealogy of Economy and Government*, trans. Lorenzo Chiesa (Stanford: Stanford University Press, 2011), 15.

45. Giorgio Agamben, *Opus Dei: An Archaeology of Duty*, trans. Adam Kotsko (Stanford: Stanford University Press, 2013), 8.

at the same time in the liturgical act—understood as *opus Dei*—mystery and ministry, that is, of making the liturgy as effective soteriological act and liturgy as the clergy's service to the community, *opus operatum* and *opus operantis Ecclesiae*, coincide.[46]

This coincidence, Agamben explains, is an ingenious and far-reaching invention of the Christian religion, which made it possible that systems and institutions—political, economic, educational, and otherwise—employed people whose will and actions integrally coalesced with that of the institutions and systems themselves.[47]

It is evident that these thoughts entail a thorough criticism of the Christian faith, both theoretically and with regard to its practical implications. Among other things, Agamben suggests that many developments in contemporary cultures—not to mention secularism in politics, economy, and private life—have a hidden, but ineradicable, genesis in Christianity. The suggestion is that to secure common and current forms of Christianity is simultaneously to endorse the environment which seems hostile to it. On the other hand, however, this intriguing critique enables one to rediscover and explore with renewed vigor the truly and fundamentally eschatological dimension of the Christian religion. For it is precisely through this dimension that faith can distinguish itself from culture, politics, economy, etc.

Agamben urgently warns the church that she should always keep and live up to the eschatological difference with any place and time where she takes root. In other words, the church

46. Agamben, *Opus Dei*, 19.

47. Agamben, *Opus Dei*, 28: "By defining the peculiar operativity of its public praxis in this way, the Church has invented the paradigm of a human activity whose effectiveness does not depend on the subject who sets it to work and nonetheless needs that subject as an 'animate instrument' to be actualized and rendered effective."

needs to reconnect with its untimely or anachronistic nature, which makes it possible that she can desacralize what is necessary and thereupon sanctify everything. However, Agamben realizes, "it is precisely this tension which seems today to have disappeared. As a sense for an economy of salvation in historical time is weakened, or eliminated, the economy extends its blind and derisive dominion to every aspect of social life."[48]

Concluding Observations

This chapter has attempted to overcome the stereotypical and antagonistic view of the relationship between liturgy and secular cultures by focusing on the theological core of the actual celebration and performance of liturgy and sacraments. Christians need not arm themselves against these supposedly devastating influences because secularism neither desacralizes the holy rites and cult of Christians nor destroys them outright. Neither is it the case that liturgy or rite impart a general sensitivity for sacredness, though such a sensitivity still endures even in radically secular cultures and in the Christian sacramental regime as embodied in liturgy. The detour around eschatology presented in this chapter made it clear that there is a fundamental difference but not an insuperable opposition between liturgy and the world. This difference can best be imagined as a creative and necessary tension. Correspondingly, the nature of the relation the liturgy always entertains (and should keep) with the world is one of inviting, embracing, and including it into the grand sanctifying dynamic which is rooted in God's revelation and redemption.

It has become clear that the eschatological dimension of the liturgy is an indispensable interpretive key in dealing with the difference between the sacred and the secular. This insight helps one understand that the worship practices of Christians

48. Agamben, *The Church and the Kingdom*, 35.

do not simply side with the sacred. Moreover, inasmuch as they tend to be focused with keeping up an unworldly sacrality rather than sharing in the divine sanctification of the world, they need to be desacralized or, indeed, secularized. Reversely, if liturgies tend to simply coincide with natural rituality—whatever that may be—it needs to be torn away from nature and reconnected with the supernatural, not suddenly and massively but gradually.

One can find such a balanced view in the work of Geoffrey Wainwright, who talks about the importance of avoiding "the danger of an ideological sacralization" and "the risk of degenerating into ideological secularism."[49] The real problem, I would add, is not the sacralizing or the secularizing, but *ideology*.[50] And that ideology can, perhaps paradoxically, only be overcome inasmuch as there is room for eschatology.

> The eschatological *reserve* requires the distinction between sacred and secular or profane. The eschatological *hope* promises that the distinction will prove to have been temporary. The eschatological *gift* already forbids an absolute separation between sacred and secular or profane and provokes even now their interpenetration.[51]

That eschatology is above all embodied in the liturgy, which is the reason one should rediscover it in the church-world encounter. And a fine sense for what the liturgy actually is and does can be found among the representatives of the liturgical movement, which we will discuss in the next chapter.

49. Wainwright, *Doxology*, 407.
50. See chapter 2.
51. Wainwright, *Doxology*, 405.

CHAPTER 5

Retrieving the Liturgical Movement

The assumption underlying the present chapter is that it is both useful and instructive, perhaps even normative, to seek inspiration in the works of premier representatives of the European liturgical movement when it comes to fundamental questions pertaining to liturgy and/in secular cultures. Although one could argue that the earliest voices of this movement had neither lived secularism nor estimated its eventual force or reality, they had a very deep sense of the liturgy and how it is intertwined with the world.[1] This chapter sets itself the double goal of rediscovering that sense and interpreting what it would entail for today. No doubt this is a difficult enterprise, especially if one holds on to a rigid scientific methodology. In that respect, I appeal not only to texts and sources and to constructive theological argumentation but also to the imagination. How would the pioneers of the liturgical movement imagine the role of liturgy in contemporary cultures in the West?

The above description of the present chapter's double goal brings along a genealogical and archaeological exercise of sorts, for it raises the question of the origins of the liturgical

---

1. In addition, it would not be an exaggeration to say that some figures associated with the liturgical movement would be fierce opponents to "secularism." As an example, one could think of Dom Prosper Guéranger (1805–75), who held a form of ultramontanism and was definitely not in favor of any "liberalism."

movement; its very *archè* and *genesis* are at stake. These origins can evidently not only be understood in a purely historical fashion but need to be approached *theologically*. That said, it is necessary to delve into the way in which a reflection on the metaphor of the Body of Christ has shaped the ideas of those scholars who have constitutively contributed to the liturgical movement. The first section of this chapter will be devoted to this topic. The second section is equally genealogical in the sense that it retrieves the concept of "mystery" and its relevance for an encompassing understanding of the liturgy. The third section then elaborates the "complexity" of the liturgy and explicates how and why it always eludes those who would wish to grasp it without becoming part of it. The fourth and final section of this chapter discusses the central notions of participation and solidarity and puts forward the idea that, ultimately, solidarity is a fruit of liturgy and love and not of constructivist secular ideologies. This insight into the connection between liturgy and solidarity can only be gained through participation in and reflection on the realities they embody. This very section thereby prepares the groundwork for the following and final chapter, wherein the argument is made that the liturgy ceaselessly invites its participants to act critically wherever and whoever they are.

The genealogical search for the origins of the liturgical movement will lead us primarily to Dom Columba Marmion (1859–1923), a figure whose work is usually only marginally referred to when the history of the movement is explained. However, it is clear that Marmion's impact on Dom Lambert Beauduin (and, through him, on many others) was immense.[2]

---

2. Although it is not extensively developed, the influence of Marmion is clearly attested in biographical literature about Beauduin. See Louis Bouyer, who wrote a beautiful book entitled *Dom Lambert Beauduin: Un homme d'Église* (Paris. Cerf, 2009), 29, 33ff.; Raymond Loonbeck and Jacques Mortiau, *Un pionnier Dom Lambert Beauduin (1873–1960): liturgie*

It is well known that the Benedictine monk of Irish descent and abbot of Maredsous from 1909 till his death was an outstanding spiritual guide and teacher. When Beauduin, who was already an ordained priest by that point, entered the newly established monastery of Keizersberg (Mont César) near Leuven in 1906, Marmion was the prior there. Thus, Marmion would massively influence the future generation of Benedictine monks who would be so closely connected to the liturgical movement and give actual shape to it.

1. The Body of Christ Image

A recurring theological theme among the pioneers of the liturgical movement is the image of the Body of Christ. They surmised an inexhaustible and at the same time highly applicable theological richness in this famous metaphor. They would often refer to it and further develop it in various directions. Commentators have observed that the idea of the Body of Christ was both foundational for and common to the liturgical movement.[3] The conceptual strength of the metaphor lies in the fact that it combines the ideas both of liveliness and of coherence, or of vitality and systematic consistence. It expresses a fundamental *organic* approach to reality, which comes close to thought patterns that had been developed by romantic thinkers.[4]

---

et unité des chrétiens (Louvain-la-Neuve: Collège Érasme, 2001), 48ff. The latter work is the extensive standard biography of Dom Lambert Beauduin. An abbreviated and more popularizing version of it appeared several years later: Raymond Loonbeek and Jacques Mortiau, *Dom Lambert Beauduin visionnaire et précurseur (1873–1860): un moine au cœur libre* (Paris: Cerf, 2005).

3. Robert L. Tuzik, ed., *How Firm a Foundation: Leaders of the Liturgical Movement* (Chicago: Liturgy Training Publications, 1990).

4. Joris Geldhof, "German Romanticism and Liturgical Theology: Exploring the Potential of Organic Thinking," *Horizons* 43 (2016): 282–307.

Obviously, the image of the Body of Christ is taken from the Pauline corpus of the New Testament. In his First Letter to the Corinthians St. Paul expounds:

> For just as the body is one and has many members, and all the members of the body, though many, are one body, so it is with Christ. For in the one Spirit we were all baptized into one body—Jews or Greeks, slaves or free—and we were all made to drink of one Spirit. Indeed, the body does not consist of one member but of many. . . . But as it is, God arranged the members in the body, each one of them, as he chose. If all were a single member, where would the body be? As it is, there are many members, yet one body. (1 Cor 12:12-14; 18-20)

St. Paul leaves no doubt about who that body is: "Now you are the body of Christ and individually members of it" (1 Cor 12:27). Consequently, the life of Christians is all about *being incorporated* into this body. In the letter to the Ephesians he makes very explicit the connection between Christ and his church through the metaphor of the body: "And he has put all things under his feet and has made him the head over all things for the church, which is his body, the fullness of him who fills all in all" (Eph 1:22-23). And in the letter to the Colossians he says about Christ: "He himself is before all things, and in him all things hold together. He is the head of the body, the church; he is the beginning, the firstborn from the dead, so that he might come to have first place in everything" (Col 1:17-18).

Clearly, these and related passages formed not only preferred quotations but germinated an entire hermeneutic, which allowed Marmion to understand the relation between God, his church, and the individual believer as well as the essential mediatory role of Christ. In other words, the image of the Body of Christ became central to a renewed spirituality which encompassed the entire life of the church and the faithful. Novel to Marmion's approach was that it was no longer a repetition of stereotypical themes and patterns in piety but that it instead quenched its thirst with a fundamental return to the sources of faith (a *ressourcement avant la lettre*). This spirituality moreover laid the basis for new ways in theology. The fact that Marmion's guiding intuition was so profoundly rooted in the Bible and tradition can hardly be underestimated. It gave the future liturgical movement a solid basis for renewal as well as for reform.

However, Marmion was not an exegete or a philologist. He did not do detailed research on the texts in their original languages or try to find the original meaning of expressions within their historical backgrounds. His work does not even reveal noticeable references to scholars who were doing that sort of research in his time. Instead he opted for a thorough synchronic and spiritual reading akin to what one would call today biblical theology.[5] The peculiarities of this approach deserve to be mentioned, because they are highly relevant for an approach to liturgy, too. The liturgy, like the word of God in the Bible, is not in the first instance a relic of the past or an object for study. Surely the liturgy and the word of God are also this, but first and foremost they are a reality to live in and to live from.[6] This, at least, is something Marmion himself lived to the full and which was deeply appreciated by those who knew him and were formed by him.[7]

5. Olivier Rousseau, "Dom Marmion et la Bible," *La vie spirituelle,* no. 325 (1948): 6–20; Denis Buzy, "Saint Paul et Dom Marmion," *La vie spirituelle,* no. 325 (1948): 21–32.

6. In this context, a meaningful parallel can be drawn with what Lutheran liturgical theologian Gordon Lathrop argued about the role of receiving the Gospel in celebrating assemblies, and about how listening to the word of God has a grand potential to transform those communities. Gordon W. Lathrop, *The Four Gospels on Sunday: The New Testament and the Reform of Christian Worship* (Minneapolis: Fortress Press, 2012).

7. Bernard Capelle, "La vie liturgique de Dom Columba Marmion," *Les Questions Liturgiques et Paroissiales* 15 (1930): 22–28.

According to Lambert Beauduin, Marmion was above all else an outstanding *liturgical theologian* in the truest sense of the words.[8] Beauduin explains that Marmion was not really a pastoral liturgist in the sense that he would stand in the midst of pastoral work in the parishes or that he was familiar with the daily lives of the faithful. Rather, his natural environment was the contemplative life of monks in abbeys—which, of course, is not to say that he had no pastoral experience at all or that he was not sympathetic to the eminently pastoral importance of worship.[9] Neither was Marmion a scholar who scrutinized the history of the liturgy such as, for instance, his renowned contemporary Louis Duchesne (1843–1922). Above all, Beauduin emphasizes, Marmion sounded the spiritual and theological content of the mysteries Christians celebrate. He prayed them as much as he preached them and thereby "organically" became, himself, a living example of their meaningfulness.

This personal insertion or, better, incorporation in Christ is of course key to the idea of Christians forming church as members of the Body of Christ. This image is especially expressive, Marmion says, "because it is borrowed from life itself."[10] It is, more concretely, related to unity and harmony, as the Body can only be one body if it has different members and one head. By becoming more truly members of the Body of Christ, Christians grow in their unity and harmony with Christ himself—and through that with God of course. Marmion repeatedly

8. Lambert Beauduin, "Dom Marmion et la liturgie," *La vie spirituelle*, no. 325 (1948): 33–45.

9. To the contrary, Columba Marmion had been a parish priest and professor at the seminary in the archdiocese of Dublin before he entered the monastery of Maredsous in 1886. This is a striking biographical parallel with Beauduin's own life and cannot but have been a matter of conversation between these two striking personalities.

10. Columba Marmion, *Christ the Life of the Soul: Spiritual Conferences* (Tacoma: Angelico Press, 2012), 99.

underscores the unity between Christ and his bride, the church, and the fact that Christ is the head of the Body: "Christ is the head of this mystical body which He and the Church constitute, because He is its Lord and Master, and because He is for all His members the source of life. The Church and Christ—this is one and the same being."[11]

This awareness gives rise to profound incitements: "Let us not forget that Christ Jesus wills the holiness of His mystical body: all His mysteries come down to the firm establishment of that holiness,"[12] with the universal possibility that everyone can always and everywhere become part of them. In these mysteries, moreover, "he shows Himself as our model; but above all He wills to be one with our souls as leader of one single mystical body, of which He is the head and we are the members."[13] The incarnation and the mediatory role of Christ in the economy of salvation which is dependent on it are absolutely central for Marmion. It is Jesus Christ's humanity and divinity which makes it possible that humanity—that is, all of humankind in the past, the present, and the future—is reconciled with God. This double nature is set forth in the church.

> When He deprived men of His sensible presence, He gave them the Church with her doctrine, jurisdiction, Sacraments, and worship, to be as another Christ; it is in the Church that we can find Him. No one goes to the Father—and to go to the father is all salvation and all sanctity—except through Christ: *Nemo venit ad Patrem nisi per me*.[14]

---

11. Marmion, *Christ in His Mysteries* (Leominster: Gracewing, 2009), 17.

12. Marmion, *Christ in His Mysteries*, 20. One can think here again of what Congar said about sacredness and the Body of Christ (see chapter 4).

13. Marmion, *Christ in His Mysteries*, 23.

14. Marmion, *Christ the Life of the Soul*, 97. The Latin quotation is from the Vulgate John 14:6. The idea of the human and divine element of the church is further elaborated on the next pages of his book.

According to Marmion, the incorporation into the Body of Christ is most intimately connected with the soteriological core of Christian faith and its sacramental liturgy. He exclaims: "Oh, if we had faith in these truths! If we understood what it is for us to have entered, by Baptism, into the Church, to be, by grace, members of Christ's mystical body!"[15] Marmion moreover appeals to St. Augustine, who in his reflections on the Gospel of St. John asserts that we become not merely Christians but that we are made Christ: *Christus facti sumus; si enim caput ille, nos membra; totus homo, ille et nos.*[16]

This very reference to St. Augustine makes one naturally think of the groundbreaking scholarly work of Henri de Lubac, who emphasized the ecclesial and sacramental dimensions of the Body of Christ. To be sure, de Lubac is generally not counted among the liturgical movement but, because of his being a premier advocate of *ressourcement* in twentieth-century theology along with Yves Congar, Jean Daniélou, and many others, it is not difficult to argue that he was after a cause very similar to Marmion half a century before him.[17] That cause was motivated by nothing other than a profound awareness of the importance of one's real inclusion in the Body of Christ.

15. Marmion, *Christ the Life of the Soul*, 101.

16. Ibid. The Latin quotation is from Augustine's *In Ioannis evangelium tractatus* XXI.8.

17. In particular, it is de Lubac's strong sense for a "sacramental ontology," or, as he himself calls it, an "ontological symbolism," that I would argue connects him with the earliest liturgical theologians of the liturgical movement. For a thorough discussion of what "sacramental ontology" means, see Hans Boersma, *Nouvelle Théologie and Sacramental Ontology: A Return to Mystery* (Oxford: Oxford University Press, 2009); *Heavenly Participation: The Weaving of a Sacramental Tapestry* (Grand Rapids, MI: Eerdmans, 2011). It is a pity that Boersma's works remain virtually silent about liturgy but, as I try to show in the present chapter, his views are by no means incompatible with liturgical theology properly so called.

How, indeed, could the Church be truly built up, how could its members be gathered together in a truly united body by means of a sacrament that only symbolically contained the One whose body it was meant to become, and who alone would bring about its unity? Saint Augustine himself becomes incomprehensible, and his entire mysticism, so full of meaning as it is, evaporates into hollow formulations if, on analysing the implications of his doctrine, we refuse to recognise within it the faith of the common tradition. For him, the Eucharist is far more than a symbol, because it is most truly that sacrament *by which the Church is bound together.*[18]

In any case, thanks to Columba Marmion, the powerful idea of the Body of Christ was taken over by many a representative of the liturgical movement. A telling illustration of this fact is Lambert Beauduin's programmatic 1914 essay, *La piété de l'église*, in which he explains what it truly means for a Christian to become a member of the Body of Christ—it is as if one hears his master speaking.

As a true member, the Catholic ought to adapt himself, unite himself as intimately as possible, to the mystical body of Christ. The state of his soul, his activity, his mentality, his whole moral being, should be modelled on the intimate nature of the Church, should vibrate with the very pulse-beat of the Church. He must be not only in the Church, but

18. Henri de Lubac, *Corpus Mysticum: The Eucharist and the Church in the Middle Ages*, trans. Gemma Simmonds with Richard Price (London: SCM Press, 2006), 252. These and other findings of de Lubac's scholarly work will make him famously conclude that the church makes the Eucharist and the Eucharist the church. See also *Corpus Mysticum*, 260 and 88, and the fourth chapter of his inspiring *Méditation sur l'Église* (*The Splendor of the Church*).

of the Church, live from the fullness of her life, be cast in the same mould.[19]

From the outset it was clear that the Body of Christ did not and could not coincide with any human association. After all, it is a *mystical* body. Marmion and Beauduin draw a clear distinction between the visible aspect of the church—its hierarchical order—and its invisible and mystical core. Evidently, the unity with Christ is not realized in the visible realm. However, without the visible reality there is no relation (possible) with the supernatural realities of grace and salvation.[20] Secularization processes may have made it more difficult to become aware of the invisible and supernatural essence of what is at stake in the Body of Christ, yet they have not made it impossible for they are incapable of achieving that entirely. The very gift of God's grace and its continuation in and through the liturgy and the sacraments cannot be made undone; it is only the conditions under which one receives it that have changed.[21] But these conditions themselves can and will change, and if the liturgy has a purpose, it is not just to add accents to these changes but to accomplish their full transformation.

19. Lambert Beauduin, *Liturgy the Life of the Church*, trans. Virgil Michel (Farnborough, UK: St Michael's Abbey Press, 2002), 32.

20. Marmion, *Christ the Life of the Soul*, 93: "It is true that the invisible Church, or the soul of the Church, is more important than the visible Church, but, in the normal economy of Christianity, it is only by union with the visible society that souls have participation in the possessions and privileges of the invisible kingdom of Christ."

21. Besides, it was the same image of the Body of Christ that inspired Beauduin later on in his life to get started with ecumenism. See Loonbeek and Mortiau, *Beauduin visionnaire et précurseur*, 146ff.

2. Mystery and Liturgy

When searching for the soul and the sources of the liturgical movement, the second striking factor is the conviction that the liturgy contains, expresses, communicates, shares in, and sets forth nothing less than the paschal mystery itself. Supporting evidence for these ideas came from meticulous historical and philological investigations undertaken, among others, by Dom Odo Casel (1886–1948) from the abbey of Maria Laach in Westphalia. His theory of *Mysteriengegenwart*, the presence of mysteries, profoundly influenced the course of liturgical studies and sacramental theology over the course of the twentieth century.[22] In particular, Casel rediscovered the rich meaning of the concept of "mystery" as it was understood by the fathers of the church, and which had somehow been obscured by ulterior interpretations of the word *sacramentum* (not to mention the scholastic theories and classifications of the sacraments). Casel observed that "Christians, even in the oldest translation of the Scripture, used the word *sacramentum* where μυστηριον could not be translated. So *sacramentum* took on the whole range of meaning μυστηριον had had."[23] Casel, then, aimed at reconnecting with the original meaning of mystery, thereby broadening the spiritual and theological content of "sacrament" and opening new paths for theological research and thinking.

22. In this context it is worth mentioning that Josef Ratzinger called Casel's mystery theology the "*vielleicht fruchtbarste theologische Idee unseres Jahrhunderts*" (probably the most fertile theological idea of the twentieth century) in a text which originally appeared in 1966. Josef Ratzinger, *Die sakramentale Begründung christlicher Existenz*, ed. Josef Ratzinger, *Theologie der Liturgie*, Gesammelte Schriften XI (Freiburg: Herder, 2010), 197–216, 197.

23. Odo Casel, *The Mystery of Christian Worship*, ed. Burkhard Neunheuser (New York: Crossroad, 1999), 56.

However, it is again to Dom Columba Marmion to which one can and should look to better understand the awakening of the awareness of the mystical core of the liturgy. This is especially evident in his collection of spiritual talks, *Christ in His Mysteries*. And again, it is a reflection instigated by the letters of St. Paul that urged him to the insight that the liturgy is necessarily linked to the mediation of the saving mysteries of Christ. In the letter to the Ephesians one reads:

> Surely you have already heard of the commission of God's grace that was given to me for you, and how the mystery was made known to me by revelation, as I wrote above in a few words, a reading of which will enable you to perceive my understanding of the mystery of Christ. In former generations this mystery was not made known to humankind, as it has now been revealed to his holy apostles and prophets by the Spirit: that is, the Gentiles have become fellow-heirs, members of the same body, and sharers in the promise in Christ Jesus through the gospel. (Eph 3:2-6)

This very passage, where the concepts of the mystery of Christ (*mustèrion tou Christou*—v. 4) and the becoming-body with him (*sussôma*—v. 6) are so neatly intertwined, was no doubt a major source of inspiration for Marmion.

The mystery of Christ, so this passage further teaches, has its origin in God's revelation. Therefore, it is not the result of human reflection or the mere outcome of the imagination. The mystery of Christ is transcendent and supernatural by essence as much as it reveals itself and makes itself in its unfathomable variety of dimensions accessible to humankind. In other words, the mystery of Christ is multiple and transparent: it is made to be stepped into, and that can be done "in many and diverse ways." God's grace and salvation are made available through these mysteries, which are one and many at the same time. "Though it be always the same Savior, the same Jesus, laboring at the same work of our sanctification, each mystery nevertheless constitutes for our souls a new manifestation of Christ; each has its special beauty, its particular splendor, as also its own grace."[24]

Marmion goes very far in stressing that Christ's mysteries are by no means alien to humankind; he even says "that the mysteries of Christ are more our mysteries than they are His."[25] By this he means that, through the incarnation and the concrete involvement in human nature, Christ becomes so familiar with human beings that nothing of what is human remains strange for Him—a reality which the tradition expresses, among other things, with the idea that He took upon Him all our sins. And because Christ became so familiar with us, it is possible to traverse this path in the opposite direction and to become familiar with Him. That, at least, is what the life of a Christian should be after: "The more we know Christ, the more deeply we fathom the mysteries of His Person and of His life, the more we prayerfully study the circumstances and details that Revelation has confided to us—the more also will our piety be true and our holiness have solidity."[26]

The most appropriate way to do this effectively is through liturgy, that is, through a life that becomes worship, which is more encompassing a reality than can be mediated simply by worshipping from time to time. The calling of a Christian is to appropriate the mystery, mysteries, of Christ. And that is always more than a simple act of remembering.

> It is therefore true to say that when we contemplate in their successive order the different mysteries of Christ, we do so not only for the purpose of recalling to our minds the events accomplished for our salvation and of glorifying God for them by our praises and thanksgiving; not only so that we may see how Jesus lived and seek to

24. Marmion, *Christ in His Mysteries*, 27.
25. Marmion, *Christ in His Mysteries*, 18.
26. Marmion, *Christ in His Mysteries*, 10.

imitate Him, but as well as this, with the object that our
souls may participate in a special set of circumstances of
the sacred humanity and may draw forth, from each of
those circumstances, the specific grace it has pleased the
Divine Master to attach to it by meriting that grace as
head of the Church, for His mystical body.[27]

However, it was Odo Casel who pointed out the extreme
importance of the concept of mystery for understanding the
liturgy theologically. In his abovementioned groundbreaking
collection of studies *Das christliche Kultmysterium* (*The Mystery
of Christian Worship*), he boldly defines the content of the mystery of Christ as follows: it is "the person of the God-man and
his saving deed for the church; the church, in turn, enters the
mystery through this deed,"[28] hence stressing the katabatic
and anabatic movements of liturgy. In a way which is very
similar to Marmion, the whole point of *being* a Christian and
having faith is about being incorporated into this mystery,
which is primarily one of salvation and sanctification. And it
is the liturgy that offers concrete opportunities to becoming
involved in this saving mystery. Casel explicitly appeals to a
patristic understanding of the concept of liturgy. It is

not an extension of aesthetically-minded ritualism, not
ostentatious pageantry, but the carrying out, the making
real of the mystery of Christ in the new alliance throughout the whole church, in all centuries; in it her healing
and glory are made fact. This is what we mean when we
say that liturgical mystery is the most central and most
essential action of the Christian religion.[29]

For Casel, the emphasis on "action" is crucial to understand
the Christian interpretation of mystery. It is much less an at-

---

27 Marmion, *Christ in His Mysteries*, 30,
28. Casel, *The Mystery of Christian Worship*, 12.
29. Casel, *The Mystery of Christian Worship*, 27.

mosphere or a subjective state of mind than an encompassing act which endures. In the end, this act is nothing else than God's revelation in Christ:

> The last and supreme mystery of Christianity, the foundation and ultimate source of all Christian mysteries is the revelation of God in the incarnate *Logos*. . . . This mystery is, therefore, an act, but an act which flows from God's depths and is therefore an endless plenitude of being.[30]

The liturgy is what mediates this plenitude:

> When we place the words "mystery" and "liturgy" side by side, and take mystery as mystery of worship, they will mean the same thing considered from two different points of view. *Mystery* means the heart of the action, that is to say, the redeeming work of the risen Lord, through the sacred actions he has appointed: liturgy, corresponding to its original sense of "people's work," "service," means rather the action of the church in conjunction with this saving action of Christ's.[31]

Again, it is striking that Casel so strongly underscores the reality of all this. He is not referring to any pious fantasy or narrative coloring of individual experiences. To the contrary, "this special sharing in the life of Christ, both symbolic and real, is what the ancients called mystical; it is something mediate between a merely outward symbol and the purely real."[32] This and many similar assertions yet again come very close to the Augustinianism which inspired Henri de Lubac. He, too, didn't see any contradiction between mystery and reason and made a strong case for the mediatory role of liturgy and sacrament:

30. Casel, *The Mystery of Christian Worship*, 57.
31. Casel, *The Mystery of Christian Worship*, 40.
32. Casel, *The Mystery of Christian Worship*, 16.

> In short, if we could for a moment translate Augustine's
> thought into our own language, we would say that for him
> any mystery, that is to say any revealed truth, is a sacra-
> ment, that is to say a sign, and that on the other hand any
> sacrament, that is to say any sacred rite, is itself a mystery,
> that is to say broadly a truth to be understood.[33]

In conclusion of this section about the intrinsic interwovenness of liturgy and mystery, a point similar to the one made at
the end of the previous paragraph can be made. Just as there
is an inalienable soteriological (Christological and ecclesiological) core in the concept of the Body of Christ, which cannot be
claimed by human effort, there is a transcendent dimension to
the concept of mystery. Mysteries mediate revelation; they are
not contradictory to human reason (and other human faculties), to the contrary, but they never coincide with what humans have on offer or can reach. It is precisely this transcendence
which makes liturgy and mystery ultimately, but fundamentally, ungraspable and uncontrollable for any social, intellectual, or cultural construction. And there is a greater problem
with cultures and societies, secular or not, if they see this principally unknowable dimension as a threat instead of an invitation to be blessed, and beyond that, to be liberated from the
weight of what Charles Taylor aptly calls exclusive humanism.[34] The yoke of the liturgy is light . . .

3. Liturgy's Complexity

The archaeological investigation of the liturgical movement
has so far identified the complex realities of liturgy. It is complex in more than one sense. First it is complex in the sense of

---

33. De Lubac, *Corpus Mysticum*, 231.

34. See Charles Taylor, *A Secular Age* (Cambridge, MA: The Belknap
Press of Harvard University Press, 2007), passim.

multilayered and multifaceted: there are many levels, aspects or dimensions to it, which must nonetheless be seen in a certain internal coherence. One could call this the "objective" side of liturgy; it mediates one and at the same time many mysteries, engages God and humankind, and is of a composite, public, and traditional nature. Second, it is also complex from a subjective standpoint. Human beings are involved in liturgy in all their complexity, that is, not only with their minds but also with their bodies. In addition, they come to the liturgy with mental and spiritual baggage, which is a result of their situation within clusters of social, linguistic, ethnic, professional, economic, and cultural networks, and their lives are marked by complicated psychological interactions with themselves, with others, and in different kinds of communities and associations. These realities have become notoriously fluid and diverse under the influence of modernity and postmodernity. Third, the liturgy is complex because of the way it is intricately intertwined with other constituents of the Christian religion, in the first place with the history of salvation but—therefore— also with doctrine and discipline.

It is worthwhile to look at these three forms of complexity in greater detail. An excellent guide for such a journey is Dom Bernard Capelle (1881–1961), a monk of Maredsous who was elected the second abbot of Keizersberg in 1928, himself a learned scholar of the history of the liturgy and an ardent defender and promoter of the liturgical movement. Like Marmion, Capelle gave series of spiritual talks, though they generally were less speculative and more informative. One topic which he regularly addressed was the meaning of the Eucharist. Fortunately, some of them have been translated into English,[35]

---

35. Much work by Bernard Capelle appeared in the journal founded by Lambert Beauduin, *Les Questions Liturgiques et Paroissiales* (now *Questions Liturgiques/Studies in Liturgy*). In 1955, 1962, and 1967 three volumes with contributions from Capelle were published under the general title

though it is a pity that they remain largely overlooked in contemporary scholarship.

The complexity of the liturgy was a theme that Bernard Capelle repeatedly stressed, to which he immediately added that this complexity, both in theological research and in spirituality, need not give rise to confusion. In an original essay entitled, "The Complexity of the Mass and the Ordering of its Parts," Capelle begins with the following warning:

> The content of the Mass is . . . manifold. In studying it we must be constantly on our guard against misunderstandings or minimising its richness in an excessive desire to set it out too logically and to systematize it. Let us always be careful not to impoverish the splendor of the gifts of God.[36]

This warning could be taken unproblematically as wise advice for anyone who studies the meaning of the liturgy today. For it entails a clear theological vision that connects the liturgy with God before it considers it a product of historical developments (which, of course, is not to say that the liturgy is not the work of human hands).

This clear theological voice also surfaces when Capelle describes the complexity of the mysteries of Christ and the church, inasmuch as together they constitute what is at stake in the celebration of the Eucharist. Like Casel, he sees mysteries

---

Travaux liturgiqes de doctrine et d'histoire. Another important detail worth mentioning is that it was Bernard Capelle who drew the young Bernard Botte into liturgical studies. See also the latter's insightful survey of his involvement in the liturgical movement: Bernard Botte, *From Silence to Participation: An Insider's View of Liturgical Renewal,* trans. John Sullivan (Washington, DC: The Pastoral Press, 1988).

36. Bernard Capelle, *A New Light on the Mass* (Dublin: Clonmore and Reynolds; London: Burns, Oates & Wahbourne, 1961), 9.

primarily as actions, and like Marmion, he lays an equally Christological and ecclesiological emphasis.

> If we are careful not to simplify too arbitrarily the multiple reality of this sacred action and at the same time to appreciate the relative importance of its elements, the truth which will strike us most forcibly is the interrelation of the two activities: that of Christ and that of the Church.[37]

The key word here is of course interrelation. Mysteries can only be understood and explained through their intimate complexity. Capelle applies this insight multiple times, for example, when he makes sense of the classical doctrines around the sacrificial and sacramental nature of the Eucharist.

> The sacrifice and the communion are two incidents of a single mystery; by their inner nature they are mutually dependent and inseparable, they illuminate and enrich each other magnificently. We cannot isolate the theology of the communion from that of the sacrifice.[38]

Capelle's meditations on the meaning of communion also led him to interesting insights concerning the human person who participates in the liturgical celebration of the Eucharist. What nourishes the faithful is "the same bread" that unveils a "mystery of unity," in other words, an "invisible incorporation through [a] visible incorporation"[39]—something which, additionally, according to Capelle, is not only realized in the Eucharist but already through baptism. The bodily dimension of this grand mystery is particularly meaningful for him:

---

37. Capelle, *A New Light on the Mass*, 15.
38. Capelle, *A New Light on the Mass*, 51.
39. Capelle, *A New Light on the Mass*, 55.

> The vital energy of our souls is received, not invisibly
> but through a sacrament; to be more precise, by the pres-
> ence of Christ in us sacramentally and corporally. We
> must not be afraid to pronounce this word "corpo-
> rally"—we must not be afraid of the palpable materiality
> of the sacrament.[40]

Another author who conceptualized the complex nature of
the liturgy in salient ways is Dom Cipriano Vagaggini (1909–
99). His position in the liturgical movement is different than
the other authors I mentioned already, since he obviously does
not belong to the founding generation. I think, however, that
it is more than appropriate to bring him into the discussion at
this point, for he can certainly be counted among those who
ascertained the continuity of the movement from the time
before the Second Vatican Council to its aftermath—and this
on several levels, theologically, historically, and practically.

In his masterly and unequaled book on the theology of the
liturgy, Vagaggini understood and defined the liturgy as a
"complexus of sensible signs."[41] This complexus of signs and
symbols constitutes an almost limitless variety of ways to connect with the history of salvation and its culmination point,
the paschal mystery. The perspective of this history and its
economy is of paramount importance to Vagaggini, for without
it one cannot understand what the liturgy is all about. In a
language that sounds highly familiar after having heard so
many voices from the liturgical movement, he states: "The

---

40. Capelle, *A New Light on the Mass*, 57; see also 58: "We must not
spiritualize arbitrarily the Eucharist. It is in body and soul that we are
members of Christ." If one realizes the background of Capelle's development, it is no surprise that it is precisely the image of the Body of Christ
that theologically motivates these thoughts.

41. Cipriano Vagaggini, *Theological Dimensions of the Liturgy: A General
Treatise on the Theology of the Liturgy*, trans. Leonard J. Doyle and W. A.
Jurgens (Collegeville, MN: Liturgical Press, 1976), chapters 2–5.

liturgy is incomprehensible if it is not related to the Church, just as the Church is incomprehensible if it is not related to Christ, and Christ is incomprehensible if He is not related to the general plan of God in sacred history."[42] As a consequence, "the liturgy is nothing other than the expression, under the veil of sacred efficacious signs, of the mystery of salvation history, by which God sanctifies men [*sic*] in Christ and by which men in Christ render their worship to God."[43]

Capelle would add that God's plan of salvation is geared towards reconciliation and unity and that it moves through the *saecula* as the mystery of love, which is indeed a "mystery of complex unity. We are all one, because all are one in Christ; and by the very fact that we are all one in Christ, we are all one with God."[44] In doing so, even if he does not make explicit reference to it, Capelle seems to recall the vocabulary and the ideas of certain medieval mystical authors expressed through it. For Bernard of Clairvaux and Jan van Ruusbroec, among others, the word *complexus* (or *amplexus*) was etymologically as well as symbolically connected with the idea of embracing: Christ and the church embrace each other as bride and bridegroom, and God embraces humankind in an act of inexhaustible love.[45]

The major reason it is so important to underscore the liturgy's complexity is that this is an ideal way to prevent it from being reduced to or exclusively interpreted in terms of other realities. Reductionisms are indeed a significant threat for theologians of the liturgy, and they can be of different kinds. To

42. Vagaggini, *Theological Dimensions*, 18.
43. Vagaggini, *Theological Dimensions*, 158.
44. Capelle, *A New Light on the Mass*, 62.
45. One would find occurrences of this language in Bernard of Clairvaux's *Sermons on the Song of Songs* and in Ruusbroec's *Die gheestelike Brulocht*. William of Saint-Thierry would be yet another author in whose work this imagery occurs.

begin with, there are reductionist tendencies both within theological circles and outside of them. These reductionisms can be motivated by methodological as well as by ideological concerns: to simplify reality and to see only things that fit is a seduction for any scholar in any discipline. But especially if the object, or victim, of one's reducing strategies is not born out of a lack of knowledge but out of a plenitude of being, it is decidedly wrong to pursue them. Inasmuch as secularist patterns of thinking and organizing operate within the scope of reductionist scenarios and exclusivist agendas, they will do no good to liturgy. Conversely, however, precisely because of its complexity, liturgy is entitled and capable to always do good to secularity. This asymmetry seems to intrinsically belong to the essence of the liturgy, its objective shapes, its subjective appropriations as well as its being-engrafted in the history of salvation and, thereby, God's embrace.

4. Solidarity and Participation

The ideas set out in the previous sections of this chapter are likely to make one look differently at the issue of participation, which is often—and rightly—considered to have been the major concern of the proponents of the liturgical movement.[46] Their case for a broader and a deeper participation with and into the liturgy was not primarily an emancipatory discourse for the liberation of laypeople. If this latter characteristic is understood in epistemological and ideological ways, it risks missing the whole point of solidarity with Christ and humanity. Promoting and helping realize active, full, or conscious participation is not primarily moving people from ignorance to knowledge, from passivism to action or from negligence to

---

46. Jozef Lambeis, ed., *The Active Participation Revisited*, Textes et études liturgiques 19 (Leuven: Peeters, 2004).

responsible functions. Rather, it is letting grow the amazement for and insight into the mysteries of Christ and His church. This is not unimportant, especially in a context of further secularizing cultures. For while these secularization processes may continue, they should not affect the deep core of Christ's love and the universal solidarity which the church is called to establish and maintain always and everywhere.

Reflecting on the genealogy of the liturgical movement is helpful, if not indispensable, to restore focus on the reality in which one participates and shares through celebrating liturgy and to put aside the maniacal theoretical adaptations which only ever attempt to access its contents. It remains, of course, very important to clear the many ways towards liturgy—and there are surely obstacles to be removed—but there are limits to the subjective accommodations one has to make. For in the end it is not certain that they better serve the goal and the role of liturgy in culture and society. To discern what this goal and this role are, the real, objective, the official and hierarchical essence of the liturgy must be brought to the fore more prominently and with more creativity. However, this requires some degree of audacity and perseverance, values which the founding generation of the liturgical movement not only held in high esteem but which they also embodied.

There is much to say in favor of the suggestion that active participation is first of all about the mystery of solidarity of Christ and the church and only secondarily about strategies of enhancing people's experiences with concrete liturgies. To be sure, one cannot have the one without the other, but that is only a pragmatic way to look at the relationship between both. Principally, that is to say theologically, the issue of solidarity is prior. There is already solidarity before one can come to partake in it, just as there are already love and redemption before one can become aware of them, and as there is a mystical and transcendent kernel in the organism of the Body of Christ before subjects can get vitally involved in and inspired by it. It is a kind of solidarity that mere human conventions and agreements can never attain. No matter how powerful, stable, and caring their capacities for community-building may be, human beings will not be in communion as they are in the sacramental communion the liturgy offers.

The offering of this communion, however, the real participation in it and the solidarity which it brings along, is the greatest gift of Christians to people living in secular environments. For it is something "other" that secular logics cannot grasp and do not have to grasp. These secular logics are redeemed from the pressure, the constant demand to grasp, and from the fact that they are seen as weak and wanting if they are unable to attain this goal. Instead of infinitely perfecting or refining this grasping, there is a way out: the way of a true solidarity for which one does not have to take the initiative oneself.

Upon close inspection, the representatives of the early liturgical movement were rediscovering these deeper layers of the meaning of participation. Clearly, for Odo Casel, participation in the liturgy is primarily motivated on theological grounds. Its very basis is nothing else but baptism:[47]

> How does this participation come to be? How does a man [*sic*] become a member of Christ? In the last analysis every participation is the work of God's grace and of eternal predestination. Upon this grace rests the first beginning of salvation's way, faith. But there is not yet the incorporation into Christ's mystical body; baptism gives this; at baptism, for the first time, the Christian meets the mystery of worship.[48]

47. For Marmion, baptism is both "the Sacrament of Divine adoption" and "the Sacrament of Christian initiation." See *Christ the Life of the Soul*, 152–58.

48. Casel, *The Mystery of Christian Worship*, 14; see also 48: "From thence it comes that the whole church, not merely the clergy is to take an active part in the liturgy, each according to sacred order, in his proper rank, place,

Lambert Beauduin concurs: "Active participation in the liturgical life of the Church is a capital factor in the supernatural life of the Christian. We found evidence thereof in the organic life of the Church."[49] Through the liturgy, Beauduin holds,

> Jesus Christ fulfils the work of His priestly mission; the Holy Spirit acts on souls; the Church puts into play the full efficacy of her priestly powers: in them we reach the source of supernatural life. The more we participate, with body and soul, the more we draw life from this source.[50]

For Marmion, the participation in Christ and solidarity with the Church constitute the very substance of Christianity.

> We shall understand nothing—I do not say only of perfection, of holiness, but even of simple Christianity—if we do not grasp that its most essential foundation is constituted by the state of a child of God; participation, through sanctifying grace, in the eternal Sonship of the Word Incarnate. All the teachings of Christ and of the apostles come down to this truth; all the mysteries of Jesus aim at establishing in our souls this wonderful reality.[51]

"But that truth," Marmion asks rhetorically, "isn't it a dream, a figment of fancy? Is it indeed a reality?" The answer to that question is simple and straightforward: "Yes, it is a reality, a divine reality" received by faith.[52] It is a liturgical reality, a

---

and measure. All members are truly, sacramentally conjoined to Christ their head; every believer, because of the sacramental character he received in baptism and confirmation, has part in the priesthood of Christ the head."

49. Beauduin, *Liturgy the Life of the Church*, 19. The famous quote from Pius X's *motu proprio*, which Beauduin had cited in his 1909 speech, is on page 50.

50. Beauduin, *Liturgy the Life of the Church*, 71.

51. Marmion, *Christ in His Mysteries*, 64.

52. Marmion, *Christ in His Mysteries*, 13.

reality which Vagaggini, in the same vein as Marmion, equals with "Christ."

> Christ, who was immolated and is now glorious, is present; Christ, who transmits His own divine life, really and objectively; Christ, who exercises His mediation in a defined manner, under the veil of things sensible and symbolic. And there is a people officially present, the Church, a hierarchically constituted representative, which accepts Christ, His reality, His action, His mediation under this veil of sensible and symbolic things; and it is by subjecting itself to this reality, by acceptance of Christ and by its submission to Him, that it communicates with God and realizes its life.[53]

It is this continued Christological focus that the church and Christians everywhere in the world would do good to always keep in mind. It gives their attempts at solidarity with each and every form of life a secure footing. Through real participation in Christ, a sharing in people's hopes and sorrows is deepened. The "founding fathers" of the liturgical movement in Europe made a strong case that this indestructible core of liturgy, if well cherished, is the strongest warrant for a good life in any circumstance. In the midst of secularization processes, one could argue, Christian liturgy anticipates "sacraments of the new society."[54] This new society can neither be realized nor ruined by secular structures (alone). And that is a very good thing, both for secular (post-)modernity and for Christianity.

53. Vagaggini, *Theological Dimensions*, 185.
54. Rowan Williams, *On Christian Theology* (Oxford: Blackwell Publishing, 2000), 209–21.

CHAPTER 6

The Liturgy's Critical Potential

On the basis of two well-known and terminologically related quotations from Vatican II documents, one can come to
a few meaningful conclusions: if the celebration of the eucharistic sacrifice is the "source and summit" (or the "fount and
apex") of the Christian life of faith (see *Lumen Gentium* 11),[1]
and if the "source and summit" of all the church's activities is
the celebration of the liturgy (see *Sacrosanctum Concilium* 10),[2]
it follows (1) that the Eucharist occupies a peculiar place in the
whole of the liturgical and sacramental life of Christians and
(2) that the life of the faithful has something intrinsically to do
with actions performed by the church. Underlying the reflections in this chapter is the presumption that, actually, neither
of both is the case.

1. *Lumen Gentium* 11 literally states: "Taking part in the Eucharistic
sacrifice, the source and summit of the christian life, they [i.e., the faith-
ful] offer the divine victim to God and themselves along with him." The
whole section is about the involvement of the Christian faithful as members of God's priestly people in the sacramental life of the church.
2. *Sacrosanctum Concilium* 10 reads as follows: "The liturgy is the summit toward which the activity of the church is directed; it is also the source
from which all its power flows. For the goal of apostolic endeavor is that
all who are made children of God by faith and Baptism should come
together to praise God in the midst of his church, to take part in the sacrifice and to eat the Lord's Supper."

Of course, it is difficult—if not impossible—to prove these claims empirically. Moreover, if these claims are generalized or universalized without nuance, it would do serious injustice to many beautiful examples in which the celebration of the Eucharist is indeed the center of the life of a given faith community's members and their various and valuable commitments. It would be a grave mistake not to see or value such practices and mentalities. In addition, the specific genre and intent of council statements such as the ones referred to above must be taken into account. They are not descriptions of a given state of affairs in reality but instead express profound and coherent theological convictions.[3] As such, they are evocative, fundamental, visionary, and idealistic rather than concrete, descriptive, or analytical.

In any case, there is something deeply problematic with regard to the relation between, on the one hand, the status attributed to the liturgy in general and the Eucharist in particular in official documents of church authorities and corresponding theologies and, on the other hand, the real role the Eucharist plays in the life of the Christian faithful in the West.[4] It is generally believed that the phenomenon of secularism has taken on its sharpest form in the West, where the relationship between the Eucharist and culture has been most dramatized. This is an issue which goes beyond the problem of declining—some would say alarming—numbers of mass attendance in many Western countries. But one must first ask whether and

3. This insight is clearly put forward in the work of John W. O'Malley, *What Happened at Vatican II* (Cambridge, MA: Harvard University Press, 2008).

4. This point of departure seems to be consonant with the findings of a most interesting practical-theological study about "Sunday" carried out and to be situated in the contemporary French context: François Werneil, *Le Dimanche en déroute. Les pratiques dominicales dans le catholicisme français au début du 3ième millénaire* (Paris: Médiaspaul, 2010).

why this declination is truly the primary problem at all. Are such considerations not frequently led by fear for the loss of societal or cultural influence?

In the light of this broader problem, I would contend that this is not solely a problem for convinced and faithful Christians and their leaders but also for society and culture. This is a bold claim which must not immediately give rise to implementation strategies, but is an idea for further theological reflections. The foundation for such reflections could probably be sought in a shift from an epistemological mentality, which is typical of secularism, to a soteriological paradigm. That shift will occupy me in the first section of the present chapter. Second, I take up the thread of the inspiration from the liturgical movement of the previous chapter and explain through a reading of Beauduin's seminal essay, *Liturgy the Life of the Church*,[5] how the liturgy can play a proactive role in the encounter with (secular) culture. Third, I argue that this approach requires that one leaves behind a limited interpretation of the Eucharist, which is rather the embodiment of the paschal mystery than a ritual among rituals giving shape to group identity in troubling times.

1. From Epistemology to Soteriology

Reasons for this Shift

A lot can be said in favor of the position that, as a Christian, it makes only little sense to be against modernity or secularism in the name or by virtue of one's religion.[6] Secularization is an

---

5. Lambert Beauduin, *Liturgy the Life of the Church*, trans. Virgil Michel (Farnborough, UK: St Michael's Press, 2002). This edition perfectly corresponds with the 1926 and 1929 Liturgical Press editions.

6. For this idea I strongly rely on and refer to the analyses of the Belgian philosopher of religion and metaphysician Ignace Verhack in his most

irreversible cultural evolution, but this does not imply that it is an evil. Therefore, "the secular" is not something to fight against but to live with in such a way that one patiently testifies a deep drive to transform it eucharistically, just as Christians are called to transform everything (i.e., every culture, every society, every people)—themselves to begin with. Perhaps too much theological energy has been spent on the question of whether to combat or embrace secularism, depending on one's initial place in the continuum described above. Paradoxically, it may well be that this often polemical—and therefore ideological[7]—work has actually overlooked the Eucharist itself as the primary source of theologizing.[8] One was so occupied by the context that one ran the risk of forgetting the content.

The reflection about apt strategies to deal with one's surroundings is only part of the job of theologians. I suggest that the time has come to pass beyond these ossified discussions about modernity and/or secularism's legacy and to intensively look at the core of what the Christian faith has to offer. This

------

recent book, *Wat bedoelen wij wanneer wij God zeggen?* (What do we mean when we say God?) (Kalmthout—Zoetermeer: Pelckmans—Klement, 2011). This intuition seems also to be shared by Charles Taylor, who defends the idea that modernity has accomplished a lot for humanity that is certainly not against the core of the Christian faith. According to him, one can even argue that some typically modern elements are dependent on a historical evolution within which Christianity was indispensable and to which it hence substantially contributed.

7. I interpret "ideological" here in a very broad sense, whereby the thought-frames that aim to deconstruct ideologies are also included, for the dismantling of ideologies is never an ideology-free maneuver. See chapter 2.

8. For a strong interpretation of what it means to see the liturgy as *primary* theology, see Alexander Schmemann, *Introduction to Liturgical Theology*, trans. Asheleigh E. Moorehouse (Crestwood, NY: St Vladimir's Seminary Press, 2003); Aidan Kavanagh, *On Liturgical Theology* (Collegeville, MN: Liturgical Press, 1992); and David W. Fagerberg, *Theologia Prima: What is Liturgical Theology?* (Chicago, IL: HillenbrandBooks, 2004).

implies, however, a thoroughgoing change of perspectives, from a focus on the weakness of the faith to its strength, from an apologetic attitude to an invitatory mood, from taking precautions to courage, and from a general sphere of mistrust to confidence. In this regard, Christians today should not build up too many illusions; just like so many centuries ago, the faith will remain foolish for the Greeks and a stumbling-block for the Jews. Then and now it is most uncertain that those who desire concrete demonstrations, whether in the form of tangible signs or invisible wisdom, will be easily served.[9] As I have extensively argued in previous chapters, cultural evidence is not (always) a blessing, let alone an indication, for the faith's authenticity.

To make the consistent focus on the core of the faith possible I think that a fundamental shift of emphasis needs to occur. I have called this a shift from a primarily *epistemological* framework to an encompassing *soteriological* look at things.[10] Contemporary cultures in the West seem to be biased by a basically epistemological attitude towards reality. On a very large scale, and in many domains of the life-world of people, there is a primacy of knowledge and the desire to know. But the question can be raised whether a cognitive interest and notional outlook are ultimately entirely satisfactory. I think that this is not the case. Cognition is important, even indispensable, and good knowledge is always rationally structured, communicable, accountable, transparent, and well-founded—there is no doubt about that. But knowledge and the corresponding human faculties of intelligence and reason may not touch the deepest layers of existence. Questions of meaning and meaningfulness, of happiness and life-orientation, of the good and its realizability, of hope and trust, of joy and misery and how they are

9. See 1 Cor 1:22-23.
10. See chapter 2.

existentially addressed, etc. can only partially be answered through *episteme* and its *logos*.

Something "more" or something "else" is needed to complement the prevailing status of the epistemological in secular cultures. That is the soteriological. Soteriology, to be sure, is not diametrically opposed to epistemology but surpasses it both in the downward and upward directions. The questions it provokes pierce deeper than mere knowledge can surmise or express, and the "answers" it provides reach higher than the culmination of cognition. The perspective of the soteriological is neither limited by rational standards nor conditioned by the a priori reasoning of autonomous subjects holding on to a methodological atheism. It aims to satisfy the whole existence of real persons, both individually and insofar as they are members of communities. If knowledge, science, technology, and reason can help persons live their lives, that seems to be fine, but if for some reason they run ashore, soteriology transcends epistemology's painful silences. Soteriology is concerned with the life-giving Word spoken by the Father, the Son, and the Holy Spirit.

The God-question, which seems to have been generally put aside in secular cultures, although from a theological perspective God continues to be (publicly) relevant,[11] serves indeed as an ideal illustration to explain the distinction between epistemology and soteriology. Inasmuch as secularism is penetrated by epistemological preoccupations, it above all wants to know whether God exists. The decision about this mostly depends on difficult reasonings and arguments but often does not leave the level of the theoretical.[12] What is worse, however,

---

11. See Jürgen Moltmann, *God for a Secular Society: The Public Relevance of Theology* (Minneapolis: Fortress Press, 1999).

12. In this respect, I think that Verhack's contention is right that it has gradually become useless, not to say ineffective and sometimes even counter-productive, to defend and explain Christianity's claims and

is that the faith commitment of many secularized people some-how depends on the certitude of whether or not God exists. Correspondingly, a believer is defined as someone for whom the assertion "God exists" still more or less makes sense. How-ever, this eagerness to know has somehow reduced faith to a set of convictions or a system of ideas, whereby the subject involved first assesses their truth-value and is only afterwards willing to consider him- or herself a believer, and only on the basis of that personal reflection process, possibly, as a member of a faith community. Both believers and unbelievers, insiders and outsiders, theologians as well as atheists, have actually stepped into this logic. But the real wealth of faith does not lie in a defensive and a priori approach.[13] When Christians ap-proach "the secular" apologetically, they in fact subscribe al-ready to polarizing schemes of thought which are at odds with their fundamentally reconciling attitude and peaceful access to reality.

As a mere assertion, "God exists" is a very meager, not to say hollow insight, though of course not an unimportant one. What does it mean to predicate "existence" of God? Is God aptly dealt with in the grammatical and logical structure of a subject to which properties can be attributed? Is existence a property next to other possible properties? It seems that tiring intellectual debates about these and related questions have

belief contents by relying on the kinds of deisms and theisms developed in the seventeenth and eighteenth centuries (*Wat bedoelen wij wanneer wij God zeggen?*, 21–29). This strategy may have proven to be successful for some time, but it certainly will no longer work in the future. For, indeed, there are only very few people who have become Christians solely through admitting that an argument in favor of theism is correct.

13. For suggestions of what, then, a "speculative a posteriori approach" may be, some inspiration can be drawn from the work of nineteenth-century romantic and idealistic thinkers like Friedrich W.J. Schelling and Franz X. von Baader. See my *Revelation, Reason and Reality*, 91–95.

had their best time—hence the proposal for a shift from an epistemological interest to a soteriological paradigm.[14] That is, one not based on discerning degrees of probability and making judgments but one inspired by what is really at stake in God's salvific initiative as it is embodied in the Christ-event and carried on through the ages by the close and mutually fertilizing entanglement of church and Eucharist.[15]

Differences between the Epistemological and the Soteriological

The soteriological differs from the epistemological in several aspects. First, it does not begin from a logic of division. Epistemologies divide, since they want to strictly demarcate what can be known from the unknowable. These divisions, however, frequently lead to divorces and separations of things which intrinsically (or naturally) belong together. What about the human and the divine, for instance? If one can gather knowledge about the human but cannot know anything whatsoever about the divine, how is one then supposed to understand things like faith, liturgy, and redemption?

Second, the soteriological is interested in *all human beings* beyond the distinctions made to organize human life-worlds and societies (like female-male, master-server, employer-employee, black-white, etc.). Soteriology is likewise interested in the *human being as a whole*, i.e., not only in intelligence and the will (as corresponding to Immanuel Kant's *Critiques* of pure and practical reason), but also in desires, the senses, passions, emotions, im-

14. It should be repeated, however, that I don't think that there is a direct opposition between epistemology and soteriology. Soteriology does not deny (the importance of) epistemology; it rather broadens and deepens its scope, or adds to it while retaining the value of what it contributes.

15. One could think here again of the work of Henri de Lubac. See also chapter 5.

pressions, etc., but maybe above all, in the imagination—a human faculty which, undeservedly, has been far too little-trusted in the history of Western thought.[16] In the end, moreover, one should always remember that the heart is more important than the head.

Third, soteriology is obviously more directly connected with the center of Christian faith than epistemology. That center, I would claim, is constituted by the Eucharist as the symbolic bearer of the paschal mystery,[17] from which everything Christians do flows forth and towards which everything they do and think is oriented (see the above quotations from *Lumen Gentium* and *Sacrosanctum Concilium*). The celebration of the mysteries, trying to realize the good, prayer (both communal and individual), and being continuously (in- and re-)formed by Bible and tradition: those are the pillars of the Christian life of faith.[18] The energetic dynamic between them is held (and meant) to draw women and men always closer to the ultimate reconciliation with God. Doctrines are essentially there to sustain and explain the living faith and customs of the tradition. But the living faith of the tradition (the soteriological) clearly prevails over its explication (the epistemological). It seems to

16. See also Douglas Hedley, *Living Forms of the Imagination* (New York: T. & T. Clark, 2008).

17. It is no coincidence that this concept has increasingly come to be seen as the fundamental category denoting the essence of Christian liturgy. See Winfried Haunerland, "Mysterium paschale. Schlüsselbegriff liturgie-theologischer Erneuerung," in *Liturgie als Mitte des christlichen Lebens*, Theologie im Dialog 7, ed. George Agustin and Kurt Kardinal Koch (Freiburg: Herder, 2012), 189–209; Simon A. Schrott, *Pascha-Mysterium: Zum liturgietheologischen Leitbegriff des Zweiten Vatikanischen Konzils*, Theologie der Liturgie 6 (Regensburg: Friedrich Pustet, 2014).

18. I am referring here to the four major sections of the *Catechism of the Catholic Church*, of which John Paul II said in the apostolic constitution, *Fidei depositum*, which introduces the universal catechism, that they are inextricably connected.

me that secular cultures have reversed this order and that therein lies the fundamental reason they alienate themselves from religion—either willingly or unwillingly, either aggressively or ignorantly.

2. The Liturgy Facing Timeless Contemporary Problems

Dom Lambert Beauduin was aware of a deep crisis within the church he had come to know better and love more fervently as he became a priest and a monk. In Beauduin's analysis, this crisis was not due to one single superficial cause, which would be fairly easy to grapple with. Rather, the problems were incisive, multiple, and encompassing. According to Beauduin, the crisis could best be felt in the church's liturgy. He was convinced that the liturgy was the most important realization as well as the most central expression of the church's very being. He even went so far as to identify the liturgy with *the life of the church*, as Dom Virgil Michel's translation of *La piété de l'église* quite rightly indicates.

The different dimensions of the liturgical crisis could be briefly described as follows. Generally speaking, there seemed to be a lack of order, or in other words, chaos. This implies that the coherence between the core and the periphery was disturbed, that one had become indifferent to what is essential, and that one attached great weight to mere details. Concretely, the proper balance between the celebration of the Eucharist, the liturgy of the hours, the sacraments, and the sacramentals had become diluted.[19] Devotions of many different kinds and intensity had practically overgrown the liturgy, with the risk of the latter being suffocated.[20] According to Beauduin, for whom the

19. For a concise discussion of this fourfold composition of the liturgy, see Beauduin, *Life of the Church*, 10–12, 58.

20. Bouyer describes Beauduin's program, which was very much influenced by his own experience, as follows: "[Beauduin] came to find his

liturgy was the *official prayer of the world church*, this was profoundly problematic. Parasites needed to know their rightful place; there was doubtlessly a lot of weeding to be done. The *order*, the right worship, or indeed the *orthodoxy*—in the sense given to it by Aidan Kavanagh[21]—had to be restored.[22]

Corresponding with the crisis observed, the envisioned restoration, renewal or reform of the liturgy was an encompassing program. One must realize, however, that the liturgical movement was not a clear operation which had set itself one exclusive goal. Moreover the objectives it did have were not to be reached through a finely delineated step-by-step approach, a clear program or a detailed schedule. The liturgy's restoration was not to be animated by a single initiative which one could copy and repeat time and again, regardless of the concrete pastoral contexts within which it had to be implemented. After all, the liturgical movement was by no means a political ideology but, instead, an authentic striving for the reform of the church and the conversion of all its members.

---

foremost liturgical apostolate in winning not so much lay people who were choir members, but first of all the priests themselves, especially the parish priests. Here is shown most clearly the perceptive genius of this great Benedictine. He himself, led by the teaching of the Pope [Pius X, to whom he time and again refers in his writings] and by his own Christian and priestly experience, had come to rediscover the liturgy as the prayer and worship of the Christian people. In the same way, he now realized that since the liturgy is the pastoral work *par excellence*, the pastors must be the first to be convinced of its value; they must be encouraged not only to promote the liturgy for the sake of their parishioners, but, first of all, to find in it for themselves the true source of their spiritual life and apostolate." Bouyer, *Life and Liturgy*, 61.

21. See chapter 1.

22. It is by no means a coincidence that the concept of *ordo* is also used to denote an official liturgical book of the church. However, the notion has a much broader meaning. For an adequate discussion of it, see Schmemann, *Introduction to Liturgical Theology*.

Inspired by Beauduin, I distinguish four areas in which the liturgy's proper critical potential can be observed. In exploring these, I think that valuable insights can be gained about being and becoming (always better) members of Christ's body today, so that a true eucharistic synthesis, or *communio*, is achieved. Hence, the hypothesis underlying the present discussion of Beauduin's work is that, after (more than) 100 years, they have lost only very little of their power of expression.

1. First, there is a clear opposition between everything the liturgy stands for on the one hand and any kind of individualism on the other hand. Quite powerfully, Beauduin exclaims: *"Whatever the liturgy loses is gained by individualism."*[23] In other words, whenever (and if) the liturgy no longer fulfills its true vocation of assembling God's people for praise, gratitude, and petition, the circumstances under which the self can develop itself in isolation gain in strength and influence.[24] The liturgy, Beauduin knows, is intrinsically social and collective; it gives shape to the church as a "visible organism."[25]

> From the very first centuries to our own day, the Church has ever given to all her prayer a character profoundly and essentially collective. By means of living the liturgy wholeheartedly, Christians become more and more conscious of their supernatural fraternity, of their union in the mystic [*sic*] body of Christ.[26]

For indeed, the body ultimately envisioned surpasses the limits of time and space as they are known through human beings' senses.

23. Beauduin, *Life of the Church*, 24 (italics in the original).
24. See also Beauduin, *La vraie prière*, 40: "Incontestablement, l'individualisme religieux nous a gagnés."
25. This term reoccurs at many different places; see, e.g., Beauduin, *Life of the Church*, 22, 23.
26. Beauduin, *Life of the Church*, 23–24.

As long as that day of perfection is not attained, the liturgy hence entails an uncompromising critique of individualism. The liturgy can, and perhaps should, play a role in confronting people with their arrogance and self-deceit,[27] in bringing people together, in sending people out to meet others, in inspiring them to engage with their neighbors and communities, and in reaching people who are otherwise forgotten. Very clearly, the liturgy shows that every human being is unique, worthy, and equal. Nothing less than the image of God, who, unlike human beings, loves everyone without distinction and without imposing conditions, warrants this. This image of God is beautifully reflected in the liturgy, which can be said to entail a marvelous and exemplary egalitarian tendency. Vatican II definitely realized this, when it said that there are indeed people with special functions and ministries in the liturgy, but that these by no means justify any other distinction, let alone a discrimination, between all men and women involved.[28] Dom Lambert Beauduin anticipated this idea in even stronger terms:

> Every child of the Church is a saint in the making. *Hence this [liturgical] piety is not reserved exclusively for an ascetical aristocracy*, and is not placed beyond the reach of ordinary Christians. All without distinction, from the Pope to the smallest child learning the catechism, live the same liturgy in different degrees, participate in the same feasts, move in the same cycle.[29]

27. This idea would wonderfully correspond with what Romano Guardini, that other pioneer of the liturgical movement, said about humility as the central liturgical virtue. See also chapter 1.

28. *Sacrosanctum Concilium* 32: "In the liturgy, apart from the distinctions arising from liturgical function or sacred Orders and apart from the honors due to civil authorities in accordance with liturgical law, no special preference is to be accorded any private persons or classes of persons whether in the ceremonies or by external display."

29. Beauduin, *Life of the Church*, 44 (italics in the original).

Obviously, if well understood and lived up to in the sincerest way possible, the liturgy can be a dynamic force in combating anti-social tendencies and measures from whichever angles they may sprout forth.

2. Second, the liturgy can be taken as an antidote to the spiritualizing tendencies which thrive in many different ways, both inside the walls of the church and outside of them, in society and culture at large. Under the category of "spiritual-izing tendency" one can understand any attempt to (wish to) look away from sheer matter. The liturgy definitely contains, mediates, and expresses prophetic visions, supernatural grace, and ideas about the end of time and world, but it never does so without concrete, that is, visible, signs. Without such a strong incarnational symbolism the liturgy would quickly degrade into "Gnosticism," as Lambert Beauduin would say, or another dualist fallacy. The liturgy's materiality matters: it cannot be imagined and experienced unless the places where it is celebrated, the colors, the vestments, the vessels, incense, etc., are taken into consideration. Beauduin is particularly firm on this:

> To depreciate ritual piety because it is not purely mental, to diminish one's participation in liturgical acts under the pretext of fostering a more interior life, is to withdraw oneself just to that extent also from the sanctifying action of the Church, to isolate oneself from the adoration and prayer of the Spouse of Christ, to lessen the influence of the priesthood of our Lord upon the soul.[30]

This due attention to liturgy's necessary exteriority is mir-rored in Beauduin's emphasis on the importance of liturgical books as "official" documents. It is in these books that one finds the true liturgical spirit and by them that true liturgical

30. Beauduin, *Life of the Church*, 15.

piety must be nurtured, so that it absorbs God's sacramental grace and saving efficacy always more intensely.[31] The prayer of the church does not originate from one's own individual imagination, no matter how pious and ingenious one might be, but from the worshiping tradition of generations of Christians since the apostles.

This sanctioning by official ecclesial authorities is further reflected in Beauduin's insistence on the importance of the church's hierarchy. By this, he does not refer to an arbitrary authority imposing its rules and laws on masses of unknowing though obedient people but the church's visible and ordered nature. Beauduin deplores that in his time there existed a large deficit in the sensitivity for the church's—and the liturgy's!—hierarchical dimension.[32] He makes that very concrete when he discusses the undeniable symbolic importance of "Rome": "By means of the liturgy, well understood and lived daily, Rome should occupy in the love and worship of Catholics the place that Jerusalem occupied in the love and the worship of the children of Israel."[33] Yet another instance in this same line of thought is Beauduin's decisive contempt for aestheticism. Of course, he does not disapprove of the (fine) arts in liturgy; to the contrary,[34] but he reproaches those for whom liturgical renewal is only "an interesting manifestation of the contemporary artistic and idealistic reawakening" of a certain "pious dilettantism" and "a capricious turn for the archaic."[35] This

31. Beauduin, *Life of the Church*, 31, 35, 44; Beauduin, *La vraie prière*, 37, 41.

32. Beauduin, *Life of the Church*, 30ff.

33. Beauduin, *Life of the Church*, 41.

34. Beauduin, *Life of the Church*, 59.

35. Beauduin, *Life of the Church*, 18.

merely aesthetic interest is "very secondary" and needs to be counterbalanced by genuine asceticism.[36]

3. Third, there is the subtle but penetrating issue of rubricism, which can be defined as a legalistic attitude in matters liturgical and which time and again looms around the corner. Liturgy evidently needs prescriptions for proper practice, but the due attention to them can easily slide into a disordered mentality that loses sight what the liturgy actually, most fundamentally, participates in and actualizes, God's sanctifying power.[37] In this context, it is telling that Beauduin opts for the concept of "prayer" to designate the liturgy's essence, for the liturgy obviously does not only consist of prayers, but also of readings, chant, gestures, etc.

According to Belgian liturgist André Haquin, specialist of Beauduin's life and oeuvre, it would be mistaken to interpret this as a kind of reduction. To the contrary, when Beauduin uses this register, he deliberately distances himself from any "juridico-rubrical" approach and instead sees the liturgy primarily as the place where the covenant "happens," where God encounters his people, and where the dialogue between them is ongoing in an effervescent dynamic.[38] Beauduin moreover deplored the waning sensitivity to prayer's genuine role and purpose, a situation which was deeply related to the broad and growing disregard for liturgical piety.[39] He was convinced, though, that

36. For a most interesting elaboration of the notion of liturgical asceticism, see the recent work of David W. Fagerberg, *On Liturgical Asceticism* (Washington, DC: The Catholic University of America Press, 2013). The relation between liturgy and asceticism was previously developed by Beauduin himself (*Life of the Church*, 61–74), something to which Fagerberg, strangely enough, does not refer.

37. See Beauduin, *Life of the Church*, 9, passim.

38. André Haquin, "Dom L. Beauduin et le congrès des œuvres catholiques de Malines. À l'occasion du centenaire du Mouvement liturgique belge (1909–2009)," in *Questions Liturgiques/Liturgical Studies* 91 (2010): 18–36, 25.

39. Beauduin, *Life of the Church*, 24, 34.

if and when the active participation of all the faithful in the liturgy is realized, this sad situation could be overcome.[40]

4. Fourth, the relationship between liturgy and secularism is a strained one, to say the least. These two forces are not diametrically opposed, but there are good reasons to assume that they may never coincide. I have amply discussed the complex phenomenon of secularism in previous chapters, so let me just point to what Dom Lambert Beauduin was trying to convey. It seems that he had adopted a fairly defensive attitude, although I do not think he would have gone as far as Alexander Schmemann, who asserted outright that secularism is the "negation" of worship.[41] Nevertheless, Beauduin definitely had a point when he said:

> To restrict religious life to the inner conscience and to consider it only as something secret and invisible, to suppress all religious acts completely in social and public life, to treat of God as the great Unknown of enlightened humanity—such is the anti-religious program of the enemies of Christianity.[42]

As we have already seen, Beauduin realized that liturgy must be a concrete and collective practice, no part of which can be replaced, invented or maintained by human convention alone. After all, the Body of Christ is a peculiar body which tenderly touches upon, deeply pervades, and at the same time

40. Beauduin, *Life of the Church*, 25: "It is they [the more fervent souls among the faithful], especially, who by their zeal, their active participation in the singing, by the sacrifice of their individual preferences, must restore the full vitality to the liturgical gatherings of the parish. This can well be called a spiritual work of mercy of the first order."

41. See chapter 4. At a theological level, however, I do think that there is a lot of correspondence between Beauduin and Schmemann—an issue which definitely deserves to be unraveled in greater detail.

42. Beauduin, *Life of the Church*, 28.

escapes all the logics of the world. In a certain sense, the Body of Christ is outstandingly romantic.

3. The Eucharist Vis-à-vis Secular Cultures

The next step of my reflections is the application of the above to the Eucharist as the culmination of the liturgy. For I think that the particularity of the (liturgical nature of the) Eucharist is largely misunderstood, both within and outside of theological circles. The secular, immersed as it is by epistemological instead of soteriological concerns, has penetrated religion and faith and is still continuously leaving its marks. In other words, it no longer stands at their doors, as some would probably like it to. Secularism cannot possibly be thought of as directly opposed to Christianity or as antithetical to faith. This is, among other things, clear when we describe a common and widespread understanding of what liturgy actually is.

Many people, Christians and non-Christians alike, suppose that the Eucharist is a ritual. Evidently, it is not a "rite of passage" in Arnold van Gennep's sense, but a ritual of the repetitive kind.[43] Such a rite is used for entertaining a positive relation with the godhead and/or for obtaining benefits from it. It aims at the stability of the community and functions as a place where the members of the community can refresh themselves at the source of their religion. This "epistemological" interpretation of the ritual nature of the Eucharist is not untrue, but it can never attain the profoundest layers of its meanings unless it opens up

---

43. Hence it should come as no surprise that, unlike other sacraments, the Eucharist does not really fit into a scheme which smoothly matches Christian sacramentality with the religious life-world of contemporary people inasmuch as the latter is centered around important transitional moments in their lives like birth, youth, marriage, and death. See Lambert J. Leijssen, *With the Silent Glimmer of God's Spirit: A Postmodern Look at the Sacraments* (New York: Paulist Press, 2006), 4–6.

itself to what I have called the "soteriological." What would this ritual have to do with God's universal salvific will sprouting from his eternal love if it is nothing more than a contingent and arbitrary instantiation of Christians' unavoidable bent for rituality? How would this ritual mediate God's mercifulness and effectuate grace? How could one think of it as an engine of faith beyond the boundaries of cultures, countries, and epochs?

If one adopts and applies a merely epistemological approach, the answer to these questions can only be formulated through the indication of external factors, for example, through mentioning that "*Christians assume* that the savior of humankind is present at their celebration." Regardless of whether one treats these factors with disdain or sympathy, one will always need a supplement "from within."

Put differently, the Eucharist is not a ritual among rituals. It is not simply one of the elements of a given set or a species belonging to a genus. But one can only see this on the condition that one is willing to leave behind an a priori approach and to adopt an a posteriori attitude, that is, if one is *receptive* to what the Eucharist *gives*. In this respect, I tend to make a threefold distinction, whereas many philosophers and anthropologists make a twofold distinction. In doing so, I engage myself in the classical nature-culture debate.

How and where does religion emerge in the development from nature to culture? Many thinkers assume that there is no spontaneous evolution from nature to culture but that at some point the natural development is interrupted. To this view, culture is this interruption of nature, and it is usually connected with the enigmatic origin of language. Language, after all, makes it possible for human societies and cultures to emerge. One usually identifies the emergence of culture with the birthplace of religion; animals, like nature, are a-religious (perhaps more consistently a-religious than many humans). And one presumes that primitive people are "more religious" than modern people, as if one could measure such a thing.

Interestingly, the distinction between the sacred and the profane reoccurs precisely at the point where culture and religion arise. Religion, inasmuch as it is a "cultural" phenomenon in the above described sense, is determined by flexible and variegating balances of the sacred and the profane.[44] The Christian faith, however, as the response to God's revelation, interrupts these balances as much as culture interrupts nature.[45] It installs a radically new perspective on reality as a whole, including nature and culture, the sacred as well as the profane. Nature and part of culture become creation; religion and other parts of culture should gradually transform into faith; and societies must be made supportive so that all of this can be achieved. Christians, then, are the women and men whom God has called upon to assist in making this happen; and they should invite literally everyone to join them but refrain from using power in doing so. Christians moreover remember, experience, and promise to participate in God's work of salvation at each and every celebration of the Eucharist. That is why there is neither profane nor secular for them; everything must be sweepingly modified through the most profound re-signification possible. That re-signification passes from the depth of the cross to the heights of the resurrection—it comes as no surprise that the sign of the cross is so essential for Christian worship.

If all this—or at least some of it—makes sense, what, then, should (or could) be done to turn the tide? That is probably the most difficult question. Nevertheless, I offer some practical suggestions to conclude the reflections offered in this chapter. First, I think that Christians must not always try to convince, prove, explain, argue, and demonstrate. The convincing-mode is doubt-

---

44. See chapter 3.

45. For a thorough analysis of "interruption" as a theological category, I refer to the work of my colleague Lieven Boeve, *God Interrupts History: Theology in a Time of Upheaval* (New York: Continuum, 2007), who in this respect is obviously influenced by Johann Baptist Metz.

lessly modeled after the epistemological and is basically rooted in a defensive strategy. The *testifying-mode* seems more appropriate and is more intimately tied up with the soteriological.

Second, I would make a case for renewing a truly *visionary theology*. Especially when confronted with secularism and (post-)modernity, Christians generally testify to less of the great vision they cherish. It is as if they silently agree to have their dreams smashed. A visionary and decidedly prophetic theology, however, keeps the senses and the minds focused on heaven, the *eschaton*, the ultimate horizon, the *parousia*, as the goal of all its endeavors.

Third, I think that a renewed emphasis and focus on the *heavenly liturgy* would be more than welcome. There is not only an "active participation" of all the members of God's priestly people in the celebration of the sacraments but also an "active participation" of the earthly liturgy in the heavenly one.[46] Epistemology is likely to find only difficulties when the liturgy talks of angels and saints, but soteriology can recover the deep sense of addressing them and celebrating the paschal mystery together with them.

Fourth, Christians steeped in secular cultures should engage in critical self-reflection. They should not only ask themselves whether they are doing, thinking, and saying the right things, but also what their deepest desires are. Do they really long for the Eucharist? Or are they preoccupied primarily with whether others go to mass? Is the Eucharist the real "source and summit" of their individual prayer life? Or do they live in a schizophrenic situation whereby their individual prayers have, on closer inspection, little to do with the Eucharist, the liturgical year, and the church? Does the Eucharist appeal to their imagination? Are they truly passionate about it? Or do they simply treat it according to their "own (particular) ritual"-mode?

Finally, Christians should enter into a great new pact with the arts, whereby art itself might come to be seen as more than

46. See chapter 2.

simply ornamental—that is, subordinate to liturgical, pastoral, or theological needs. The kind of art that I envision shapes the eucharistic imagination and experience. Austrian composer Peter Jan Marthé's *erdwärtsmesse* is a clear example of such a vision.[47] This magnificent piece of music does not eschew the effects used in film scores, and it must be performed by an organ, wind instruments, percussion, a baritone, a large choir and—in line with the liturgical reforms of Vatican II—the whole gathered assembly. The *erdwärtsmesse* looks secular culture right into the eyes and boldly proclaims: come and see, you're wholeheartedly invited to join into what gives us Christians the most perfect joy . . .

47. Peter Jan Marthé, ed., *Die Heilige Messe. Kultisch—szenisch—sinnlich—mystisch* (Würzburg: Echter, 2011).

Concluding Observations

When Dom François Vandenbroucke, monk of the Abbey of Keizersberg and for some time editor-in-chief of *Les Questions Liturgiques et Paroissiales*, commented only one year after the publication of *Sacrosanctum Concilium* on whether the liturgical movement had achieved its goals, he underscored the integrity and entirety of the liturgy. According to him, the real objective of the liturgical movement consisted in "rendering the plenitude of meaning to the whole economy of the Church's 'sacred signs,' and *thereby* allowing the faithful to become more thoroughly aware of their Christian vocation and to journey towards God."[1] In that order. To respect that order, however, is neither easy nor evident in a context which seems not, or no longer, favorable to the life of the soul and the quiet it naturally seeks. Vandenbroucke does not speak of secularism in so many words, but he does name "modern humanism," which could arguably explain the same reality. He then says:

> Human beings in the 20th century lose their soul, submerged as they are, even drowned, in hallucinating information, in a ravaging, feverish hurry, a literally burning activity. And the success of a new liturgy where action, community and words tend to thwart silence, the ponderings of a soul which finds in itself the Trinity, the gratuitous

---

1. François Vandenbroucke, "Réussite du mouvement liturgique?," in *Les Questions Liturgiques et Paroissiales*, no. 243 (1964): 314 (my translation, JG).

contemplation of the *mirabilia Dei*, love which is a gift, a service, a consecration, could in fact turn out to be nothing but a resignation, a pusillanimity, a failure.[2]

These penetrating observations are worthy of comment, for they could be too easily taken to mean two things which I think they do not. First, Vandenbroucke's statement could be seen as a direct criticism of the liturgical reforms issuing forth from Vatican II. Already from a simple historical point of view, this is a difficult point to make, for the reforms themselves had hardly begun.[3] It can be added that such a critique was not what Vandenbroucke intended; he rather expressed the genuine concern that liturgical reforms be in line with the theological essence of liturgy and that they not chase after temporary or fleeting fashions. Second, one could read Vandenbroucke's quote as suggesting that there is a diametrical opposition between the church's liturgy and modern life. He does see a tension between the hectic of professional and family life in secularizing cultures on the one hand, and the contemplation-oriented character of Christian liturgy on the other. Obviously, his own monastic experience and the implicit norms derived from it must have shaped his model for assessing contemporary developments. I think, however, that this is a surface-level observation, and that something more profound is going on. Vandenbroucke endeavors above all to lay his finger on the fundamental *difference* between liturgy and secularism, but he doesn't claim that there is a blatant contradiction between the two.

2. Vandenbroucke, "Réussite," 315 (my translation, JG).

3. For a survey of the historical context immediately following the promulgation of *Sacrosanctum Concilium*, see Piero Marini, *A Challenging Reform: Realizing the Vision of the Liturgical Renewal, 1963–1975*, ed. Mark R. Francis and Keith F. Pecklers (Collegeville, MN: Liturgical Press, 2007).

To interpret this difference as a non-opposition is today as challenging as it was a century ago, when the liturgical movement arose; it was no less difficult in the 1960s, when Western culture found itself on a kind of roller-coaster. However, it remains as important now as then to maintain the key conviction that the difference between liturgy and secularity does not necessitate a decision for one, and as a consequence, against the other. Liturgy escapes the anti-secular and hyper-secular dichotomy, and reversely, secularism cannot be caught by the church's liturgy. As a corollary, secularism is not a threat or a danger for liturgy. Secularism is incapable of diminishing or destroying liturgy. What remains true, however, is that secularism involves the risk of making it very difficult for persons— Christian and non-Christian alike—to convert, to open their hearts, bodies, minds, and souls to the work of redemption which is mediated by liturgy. There are also, of course, other socio-cultural and intellectual conditions under which this is laborious. It is possible that these troubles have, in the end, more to do with an intrinsic recalcitrance in human nature than with the precise circumstances in which persons become members of the Body of Christ.

Inasmuch as one can rightly interpret Dom Vandenbroucke's observations in the way I argued for, it gives us a good opportunity to look back on the trajectory this book traversed. First, I have to say something about the two mottos taken from *Sacrosanctum Concilium* that oriented the scope of the diptych. Second I recapitulate some key insights that the excursions in liturgical theology, philosophy of culture, history of ideas, and anthropology have yielded. That exercise will at the same time enable me to briefly dwell on the sources that I have used. Thirdly, I want to conclude this book with some open suggestions for further research and reflection.

1. The originality of diptychs consists in their capacity to invite people to contemplate and interiorize mysteries. Mysteries are no secrets but pervasions, maybe invasions, of transparency.

They are full of light, and truth, and goodness, and beauty and by their permanent offer of access exhibit perfect examples of non-discriminatory realities meant for everyone, everywhere, always. Sacraments are mysteries, but the very origin and principle of the liturgy, its *archè*, is no less (a) mystery. Liturgy is mystery mediated, is mysteries sacramentally carried on through the centuries to every corner of the globe.

The two paragraphs from *Sacrosanctum Concilium* each in their own way give voice to this fundamental, mysterious, sacramental, mediating essence of the liturgy. Liturgy is something of the world and of human beings, but it is *also* something of the heavenly Jerusalem; it is something which aims at the sanctification of the world, but is *also* worship of God, *cultus divinus*; it is a visible ritual activity of gathered assemblies, but it is *also* the eternal prayer of the Church, the Bride, and her Bridegroom, Christ, the High Priest. In all these phrases, the nature of this "also" needs to be well understood. It is not an addition or a culmination of elements but an organic intertwinement. Inasmuch as the two paragraphs from the council's constitution on the liturgy express and promote this intriguing reality of a universal transformative dynamics incarnated in diverse and multiple celebrations, they offer the best possible background for the points that I have been trying to make.

In sum, the two quotations from *Sacrosanctum Concilium* constitute the horizon which positions liturgy in the world and the world in the liturgy, and moreover, they offer solid theological motivations for rejecting the supposedly unbridgeable cleft between liturgy and secular culture. This division is not necessary to come to terms with the essence of Christian faith and, in particular, its redemptive promise and potential.

2. Correspondingly, this book set itself a triple objective. First of all, it aimed to demonstrate that one does not have to oppose or elbow out secular culture if one wants to make room for liturgy. We are talking about different spaces. Secularism as such is not a danger, though careful distinctions must al-

ways be made between a socio-cultural, historical, and intellectual evolution on the one hand and a political ideology on the other. Liturgy, however, because it transmits "the work of our redemption," can deal with both. Liturgy can face the challenges of cultural change, societal development, and the continuous adaptations of intellectual paradigms. Liturgy can even creatively contribute to such evolutions and accidental revolutions. If Christ is the measure, and to the extent that He can inspire by offering criteria for discernment, the contribution of liturgy and the involvement—active and conscious participation—of Christians to historical shifts is even desirable. For liturgy can entail subversive, irenic, bright, and exciting insights that undermine ideologies which run contrary to the good of creation or which obscure paths towards the liberation of people.

In other words, there is a severe incommensurability between liturgy and secularism, which is why it is so important that Christians in the West, but by extension everywhere, get beyond the divide between both. The divide between liturgy and secularism is a construction of secularist thinking not supported by a thorough reflection about the liturgy itself. It is a pity that so many philosophers, theologians, and church leaders have fallen into the trap of believing that either you defend liturgy or you become secular. Right apology for liturgy does not depend on bashing secular thinking, and one does not need a rhetoric against modernity or postmodernity, against their supposed rationalism and concomitant desacralization, to clear the way for a safe life of worship. It is much more important that the church is perseverant, authentic, and creative in continuing her mission to be *ecclesia orans* and to become the Body of Christ than that she cast blame or disapprobation at the inevitable development of culture.

Obviously, not all the sources I have consulted to build up this case were classical theological authorities; neither was the amount in which inspiration from them was drawn spread equally. One reason I have chosen to engage with philosophers, historians, and anthropologists of different schools and backgrounds in this way is the strong conviction that the liturgy in all its complexity is best served by dialogical thinking. Beautiful in itself, the liturgy is not a compact system which only requires rigid procedures for its maintenance. Liturgy is not dependent on exclusively or meticulously justified adaptations and interpretations, nor through well-defined and appropriately-planned applications designed to distinguish its practice from impermissible excursions into realms supposedly foreign and hostile to it. To the contrary, liturgy is embedded in messy realities; it is connected in ways which can hardly be imagined to the whimsical, fanciful, unpredictable, tested, and tormented lives of people, as well as to their experiences of joy and jubilation. Liturgy itself, however, is not and should not be messy and capricious. It brings (to) light and represents the otherness of the origin of all truth, beauty, and goodness. So, in order to grasp the ungraspable, there is no better way than to engage in thoroughgoing discussions with a rich diversity of scholars, with varying sympathies and antipathies towards Christianity and Christendom, and with varying competencies and opinions.

3. But where do these diverse discussions ultimately lead? What happens next, if it is true that liturgy and secularism are incommensurable? What follows once the assumption of the divide between them has been successfully undermined? For which purposes is this assumption shown to be useless and superfluous? How can the efforts of continuing the dialogue between liturgy and culture be made fertile for the future of the Christian religion? I see consequences for liturgical theology, for the life of the church, and for pastoral practice and will concisely indicate them in reverse order in order to respect their real priority.

At the pastoral level, Christians must be equipped with more daring to testify about their being immersed in liturgical celebrations. It is true that there is not always much that enters into the purview of the conscious intellect and of (religious) experience,[4] but unique or intense experiences and purely intellectual discourses are not what liturgy is all about. Liturgy is about better becoming and becoming better members of Christ, about partaking in the paschal mystery, and about ceaselessly renewing and deepening one's relation with God and with each other. Pastoral liturgical initiatives must be designed such that they, negatively, do not distract the focus from these mysterious realities, and, positively, stimulate many creative ways to form oneself in the church's matrix.

At the level of the official and institutional church, certain mentalities ought to be questioned, hidden power games unmasked, and unworthy authorities dismantled. Sadly, the Catholic Church has known for quite some time a sharp internal division between left and right, which are respective heirs of the once so-called progressive and conservative parties at the Second Vatican Council. It is highly deplorable that the liturgy has been one of the battlefields between them, for the liturgy should not be the wager of militant minds but precisely that which frees from the fight. While those on one side reproach the supposed forces of secularization, desacralization, and democratization of the liturgy, those on the other level accusations of traditionalism, anti-modernism, and of artificially alienating liturgy from the lifeworlds of ordinary people. The truth, however, is that these debates are pointless if one does not see that they rather concern styles, shapes, and customs which unravel and communicate the mysteries at the heart of Christian worship. Liturgy does not exist to upkeep an enchanted universe, nor should it fall prey to frivolous disenchantment. Liturgy is the place of simple chanting: it offers spaces where God's praises are sung in communion and

4. See the intriguing musings of Jean-Yves Lacoste, *Experience and the Absolute: Disputed Questions On the Humanity of Man*, trans. Mark Raftery-Skehan (New York: Fordham University Press, 2004).

where gratitude for His creation and redemption takes on the form of concrete charity.

For liturgical theology all of this means that the work continues. The involvement in and the reflection about liturgy can guide them anywhere, but they should always be stably situated in the Body of Christ. In the midst of contexts which are, rightly or wrongly, heavily or slightly, increasingly or decreasingly, secular, they must seek numerous ways, traditional and innovative ones, to conceptualize the embodiment of Christ's mystery in sacramental signs and to explain how liturgical celebrations of the church intensify God's engagement with the world. They will have to clarify that this is not just a story of comfort and uplifting for the weak, the discouraged, and those who do not know better. It is not just a framework of rites and symbols which try to make sense of the world in troubled times but the establishment of God's economy of salvation. It will be increasingly important for liturgical theologians to underscore the gravity of this assertion: that liturgy touches on the deepest drives of people, that it connects with the trajectory of the world, that it is rooted in the history of humankind, that it transforms reality for the good, and that all of this can be shown and, more importantly, that one can participate in it. In other words, liturgical theologians, incited by "an exuberant enthusiasm for the supernatural life,"[5] are invited to develop a veritable metaphysics: not just an explanatory sacramental ontology but an exploratory, profoundly soteriological, eschatological, and doxological Christian realism. *Ad maiorem Dei Gloria.*

5. Lambert Beauduin, *Liturgy the Life of the Church*, trans. Virgil Michel (Farnborough, UK: St Michael's Abbey Press, 2002), 28.

Index

Active participation, 1, 36, 118,
    119, 121, 139, 143, 149
Agamben, Giorgio, 41, 42–44, 45,
    46, 47, 48, 92, 93–94, 95
Alberigo, Giuseppe, 33
Angels, 16, 21, 43, 93, 143
Anthropology, xiv, xvi, 9–10, 50,
    59, 83, 147
Atheism, 81, 92, 128, 129
Augustine of Hippo, 16, 104, 105,
    111

Baldovin, John F., 7
Baptism, 84, 88, 100, 104, 115, 120,
    121, 123
Beauduin, Lambert, 21, 24, 98, 99,
    102, 106, 113, 121, 125, 132,
    134, 135, 136, 137, 138, 139, 152
Being, 24, 47, 52, 53, 56, 58, 59, 61,
    65, 66, 67, 118
Benedict XVI, 32
Bernard of Clairvaux, 117
Bible. *See* Scripture
Blood of Christ, 88
Blumenberg, Hans, 27, 63
Body of Christ, 8, 16, 24, 44, 84, 86,
    87, 88, 98, 99–100, 102–6, 112,
    116, 119, 134, 139, 147, 149, 152
Boersma, Hans, 80, 104
Boeve, Lieven, 142

Botte, Bernard, 114
Bouyer, Louis, 84, 98, 132–33
Breviarium Romanum, 5
Brito, Emilio, 60
Bugnini, Annibale, 3, 6, 7

Carr, Ephrem, 8, 30
Capelle, Bernard, 101, 113, 114,
    115, 116
Casel, Odo, 15, 71, 92, 107, 110,
    120
Catechism, 71, 131, 135
Catholicism, 10, 12, 85, 124
Chauvet, Louis-Marie, 17, 23, 71,
    87
Chenu, Marie-Dominique, 84
Christ. *See* Jesus Christ
Christendom, 11, 22, 39, 150
Christianity, 10, 23, 33, 38, 39, 62,
    65, 80, 83, 90, 92, 94, 106, 111,
    121, 122, 128, 139, 140, 150
Christians, xiv, 24, 25, 42, 43, 49,
    60, 73, 79, 90, 91, 95, 100, 102,
    104, 107, 120, 122, 123, 125,
    126, 127, 129, 131, 134, 135,
    137, 140, 141, 142, 143, 144,
    149, 150
Christology, 112, 115, 122
Church, xiii, xiv, xvi, xvii, 1, 5, 17,
    18, 19, 21, 24, 25, 30, 32, 38, 44,